John Pritchard is Bishop of Jarrow. He was Archdeacon of Canterbury and, before that, Warden of Cranmer Hall, Durham. He has served in parishes in Birmingham and Taunton and has been Diocesan Youth Officer for Bath and Wells diocese. Previous books by the author include *The Intercessions Handbook*, *The Second Intercessions Handbook*, *Beginning Again*, *Living the Gospel Stories Today* and *How to Pray*. He is married with two daughters.

LIVING EASTER THROUGH THE YEAR

Making the most of the resurrection

John Pritchard

First published in Great Britain in 2005

Society for Promoting Christian Knowledge
36 Causton Street
London SW1P 4ST

SPCK does not necessarily endorse the individual views contained in its publications.

British Library Cataloguing-in-Publication Data
A catalogue record for this book is available from the British Library

ISBN 0–281–05709–5

1 3 5 7 9 10 8 6 4 2

Typeset by Graphicraft Ltd, Hong Kong
Printed in Great Britain by Ashford Colour Press

For Wendy, loving companion on the journey

Contents

Part Three
MAKING THE MOST OF THE RESURRECTION
Courses, prayers and poetry

Acknowledgements

Biblical quotations are taken from the New Revised Standard Version of the Bible © 1989 by the Division of Christian Education of the National Council of the Churches of Christ in the USA. Used by permission. All rights reserved.

The author and publisher acknowledge with thanks permission to reproduce the following material:

p. 36, Ruth Etchells, 'Ballad of the Judas Tree'.

p. 128, W. R. Rodgers, extract from 'Resurrection', from *Poems* 1993, the Estate of W. R. Rogers and the Gallery Press, Loughcrew, Oldcastle, Castle Meath, Ireland.

p. 129, John Updike, 'Seven Stanzas at Easter', from *Collected Poems*, Penguin 1995.

p. 130, Ruth Etchells, 'Easter St John'.

pp. 132–3, David Grieve, 'Deleted', 'Eastering'.

p. 134, Val Shedden, 'Resurrection', 'Next time'.

p. 124, David Gavin, 'A week in the life of Death'.

Other poems and extracts are from the following sources:

p. 127, Veronica Popescu, 'Transcendence', source unknown.

p. 127, Elizabeth Jennings, 'The Resurrection', published by Andre Deutsch.

p. 131, Steve Turner, 'Poem for Easter', from *Up to Date*, Hodder and Stoughton 1983.

And special thanks to Ron Wood for permission to use his cartoons on pp. 2, 12, 38, 51, 66, 92, 125.

Whatever happened to Easter?

At one time my father was vicar of a large church in Blackpool. One of the sidesmen there was called Mr Wrigley. He was a quiet, no-nonsense Lancastrian who didn't say much; he just got on with his job. But once a year he came into his own. On Easter morning Mr Wrigley would walk purposefully down the length of the church to the vicar's vestry – a long journey. He would stand in the doorway of the vestry and say to my father, 'Christ is risen, vicar!' My father would reply, 'He is risen indeed, Mr Wrigley!' And Mr Wrigley would nod – satisfied – and set off for the back of the church again for the rest of the year.

I used to love that exchange. Here was this undemonstrative man bearing witness to the core belief that sustained him through his life, and kept him giving out hymn books and loving his wife and following his conscience and giving to charity and simply being himself. Mr Wrigley didn't live a spectacular Christian life. He wouldn't have known what that meant. But he knew what he believed, and it was simply this: Christ is risen! And so everything else would be all right.

Nevertheless, as I've gone on in my own Christian journey I've increasingly felt cheated by how we handle this King of Festivals. We give a great welcome to the Christ-child. We focus with fierce tenderness on Christ crucified. But Christ risen always seems to get the short straw.

Take the Christ-child first. Society prepares for him from the end of September. The Church tries to hold back the tide of commercial expectation, at least until Advent has had a bit of a run, but eventually the tidal wave overwhelms even the Church and we enter the carol-service-and-nativity-play-season with a will. Shepherds, angels and kings are all over the place. Little donkeys carry Mary. Stars twinkle over the stable if the electrician has done his job. And in the middle of it all 'the heavenly babe you there shall find', trying his best to survive the fuss.

For Christians, the heavenly babe, the Christ-child, is clearly at the centre of our Christmas celebrations. Society may allow its gaze to slip on to the Christmas tree, the credit card and the television schedules, but the Church is clear: the holy Child of Bethlehem is the focus of our joy.

Similarly, when it comes to Lent and Holy Week, Christians are clear about the direction of their gaze. We're looking towards Christ crucified. The terrible events of that most ravaging of weeks have been the source of more prayer, reflection, theology, music, art, tears and sighs than any other week in history. Mel Gibson's demanding film *The Passion of the Christ* is just one more attempt to penetrate the atrocity of those hours without flinching. And who can see the tortur-

Sir Rodney really enjoyed Easter Sunday

ing of Love without tears in their eyes? Again, this central icon of Christian faith stands out with irresistible clarity – Christ crucified fills our vision.

We travel long and hard through Lent and Holy Week. The build-up of spiritual pressure is immense. Liturgies and readings are slow and sombre, echoing the stripped décor of the churches. Then Good Friday arrives and the worst thing we can imagine begins to happen: God the most holy Trinity goes into meltdown. The evening of Good Friday is a time of almost guilty relief ('at least the suffering's over'), and then Holy Saturday is a day of spiritual exhaustion, dull, flat and colourless.

And then comes Easter Day – the most astonishing day in the history of the world. The Lord of history erupts into his own creation, shattering our closed minds and throwing open the windows of eternity. Christ is risen! There's ecstasy for a moment, sheer, wild, abandoned ecstasy.

And then we have a Bank Holiday.

That's what I can't grasp. How can we come so close to such breath-taking good news and then just wander off to the airport? How can we rise so high and then collapse so ignominiously? With all our other summit experiences we do our best to hold on to the magic, at least for a while. When we fall in love, for example, we're convinced we've solved the Problem of Life. This is fantastic. This is life in its pure, uncut form. This is what we hardly dared believe could exist. We don't just empty the bins and clean the bathroom and slump in front of the television. Life suddenly holds so much more.

But it seems that the glorious, breath-taking, mind-numbing event of the resurrection only holds us for a morning. Then we move on with what seems like unseemly haste. The liturgies and readings of the Church do their best to reflect an Easter faith over the following weeks but somehow we don't seem to have the facility to hold on to the ecstasy of Easter. It's died away before it's had a chance. Let's look forward to the summer holidays.

I was once on a retreat where the talks were being given by a very traditional figure, a priest in black cassock, properly white-haired and ascetic in appearance. He seemed to come from another age, a far-off time when clergy like this were mass-produced somewhere in Middle England and made the Christian life seem rather alarming. But he sat in front of us in one talk and simply said to us: 'In your life and ministry, never let the sorrows of this world hide from you the joy of Christ risen.' Spot on, I thought. I've carried that phrase with me for years.

My understanding of the Christian life has always been associated with 'the joy of Christ risen'. If Christ really is risen and let loose in the world then it makes a world of difference. Everything about our lives as believers is then bathed in the glow of resurrection. Every pleasure is enriched by the presence of this good Companion. Every tragedy is back-lit by the hope of an empty tomb. It seems wonderfully obvious that 'we are an Easter people, and alleluia is our song'.

I was called into hospital one night to be with a woman who was dying in middle age. Jean and her husband were faithful members of our church and I had travelled this hard road with them for some time. Of course, Hugh was there. In the early hours of the morning Jean gave up the struggle and graciously left the field, leaving behind a large, empty, peaceful space. We sat together and prayed and talked. I stayed as long as it seemed helpful. Eventually I knew it was time to leave them, and I stepped out of the hospital just as day was breaking. The mysterious light of dawn was stealing over the car park; the birds were picking out their best tunes and the air vibrated with promise. It was Easter morning. And I knew as surely as I knew my own name that Jean was secure in a Love far stronger than the ravages of death. She was in her own Easter garden, meeting her risen Lord.

That is the faith I want to celebrate in this book. I want to offer a range of thoughts, insights, resources and ideas for action that might help the willing reader to live the Easter faith long after that glorious morning is past. I don't presume that everyone will find everything in the book of equal value. But when we're dealing with something as enormous as resurrection it won't be surprising that we need a multi-layered, kaleidoscopic approach to living out the Easter faith. What I offer is a collage of material – stories, reflections, ways of prayer, poems, courses of study, quotes, music and film – all sorts of ways to keep the party going.

My concern is that we 'let him easter in us', in Gerard Manley Hopkins' memorable phrase.

I shall start with the Easter events themselves and what happened afterwards. Those are the raw materials, after all; they need to be checked out. Then I shall explore ways of celebrating Easter, both at the time and in the following weeks and months. And then I shall offer courses, prayers and poetry to keep the momentum going and embed the resurrection in our on-going life of faith.

I suspect the resurrection party has never stopped in the halls of heaven since that first amazing Easter morning. Each of us is given an invitation to join that party, indeed to start partying even now, this side of heaven. And if that sounds too exhausting to those of us who are introverts, I'm sure there are quiet ways to party as well!

But what will we write on the RSVP?

Part One

THE RAW MATERIALS
The events and their aftermath

Have I got news for you!

WHAT DO THE GOSPELS SAY?

One of the puzzles of Easter is the different stories the Gospels tell. At least in detail. They don't have any doubt about the central fact that Jesus is risen but they don't seem at all of one mind about who did what when.

For example:

- How many women were involved – two (Matthew), three (Mark), several (Luke) or one (John)?
- Had the stone already been rolled away before the women got there (Mark, Luke, John) or were the women there when it happened (Matthew)?
- How many angels were there – one (Matthew and Mark) or two (Luke and John)?
- Was there some communication from the angel(s) on the first visit to the tomb (Matthew, Mark and Luke), or not (John)?
- Did the women tell the other disciples (Matthew, Luke, John) or not (Mark)?
- Who else was at the tomb apart from the women – 'the beloved disciple' and Peter (John), the guards (Matthew), nobody (Mark and Luke)?

So it's all a bit confusing! Some people try and make a consecutive narrative out of these complexities and so smooth out the differences, but that's to miss the point. Those very inconsistencies are one of the best arguments that what we're dealing with here are first-hand accounts, passed on with care and reverence.

Imagine you're trying to get a proper account of a particularly important football match. If you ask four different people you'll probably get four very different accounts depending on the person's allegiance, their viewpoint in the stadium, their descriptive skills, their personality type, and whether they happened to be looking at their watch at a key moment! Maradona's infamous 'hand of God' goal in the World Cup quarter-final some years ago was viewed very differently by English and Argentinian fans as well as by different camera angles!

If we apply that analogy to the Gospel accounts of the resurrection we get four different 'angles' on what is clearly the same extraordinary event. *Here it may be useful to refer to the four descriptions which you will find printed in full in Appendix 1.*

- **Matthew: the view from the stands** Matthew was after the wide-angle view, the big picture. He saw the cross and resurrection in the light of the whole build-up to those events through Jewish history and through the struggle Jesus had with the Jewish authorities. He also wanted to make clear where it was all leading – the commissioning of the disciples to take the mission worldwide. Matthew saw all the corner flags on the pitch.
- **Mark: the view from behind the goal** Mark's account of the event is a direct, dramatic, no-frills match report in which unfortunately the ending of the report got lost on the way home! It ends far too abruptly for that to be Mark's intention. Endings have been added subsequently but they're not convincing. But the main body of the account is vivid, fast-moving and bustling with action. Perhaps he wrote for the tabloids!
- **Luke: the view from the media box** Luke's avowed purpose is to offer the Roman official Theophilus an authoritative and credible account of the facts concerning Jesus and his significance for the life of the world. He wants to convince, but through hard history. He's also a journalist with flair – see the lovely account of the walk to Emmaus which two disciples share with Jesus. Luke has a warm interest in the players, and as he may have had some medical training, he shows a real concern for those on the injured list.
- **John: the view from the manager's bench** John has had time to reflect on the significance of all these things and he gives us the inside view of what was happening in poignant encounters with Mary Magdalene, Thomas, Peter and John. There's inside knowl-

edge here, the strategy and tactics of the game – the kind of things only the manager and the substitutes around him get to know.

The analogy shouldn't be pushed too far, but just as a football match is inevitably seen through very different eyes, so the resurrection events were seen through different 'filters', with different elements of the story regarded as important and different parts remembered and honoured.

Let's now look at the four accounts in terms of the *scenes* they use and the *shots* each scene contains.

Matthew

Scene one: the tomb

- Mary Magdalene and 'the other Mary' go to the tomb at dawn.
- There's an earthquake; an angel announces that Jesus is not there, and sends the women to tell the disciples to go to Galilee to meet him there.
- The women run off, meet Jesus, hold on to him, but are again sent to tell the disciples to go to Galilee.

Scene two: the guards and the chief priests

- The guards report the bad news to the chief priests.
- The priests and elders assemble and come up with a plan to bribe the soldiers to say that the disciples came and stole the body of Jesus.

Scene three: a mountain in Galilee

- The disciples meet Jesus and most worship him 'but some doubted'.
- Jesus commissions the disciples to make disciples all over the world and to remember that he will always be with them as they do it.

Mark

A single scene: the tomb

- Mary Magdalene, Mary the mother of James, and Salome go with spices to anoint Jesus.

'And that's exactly what happened, sir, while we were all asleep . . . '

- The stone has already been moved and they meet 'a young man' in the tomb.
- The young man tells them Jesus has been raised. They are to tell the disciples to go to Galilee to meet Jesus there, 'just as he told you'.
- The women flee in terror, scared stiff.
- There are then two dubious endings to the Gospel, added later.

Luke

Scene one: the tomb

- Mary Magdalene, Joanna, Mary the mother of James and other women arrive at dawn with spices.

- The stone has been rolled away and two men in dazzling clothes terrify the women and ask why they are 'looking for the living among the dead'. They remind them that Jesus foretold all this.
- The women go back to tell the disciples, who basically think this is all 'an idle tale'.
- But Peter goes to check the story out, sees the empty linen clothes, and is amazed.

Scene two: the road to Emmaus

- Two disciples are wandering disconsolately back to Emmaus and are joined on the road by Jesus, whom they don't recognize. They recount the events of the last few days and Jesus explains the scriptures to them.
- They arrive at their home and ask Jesus in. He does the familiar actions he always did with bread – blessing, breaking and sharing it – and then disappears.
- They realize what has been happening and rush back to Jerusalem with the news, and find that Jesus has also appeared to Simon.

Scene three: the upper room?

- Jesus appears and tries to deal with the disciples' doubts by pointing to his hands and feet and by eating some broiled fish.
- Jesus reminds them that all that has happened was foreseen in the scriptures and declares that they are to be witnesses of it all, promising that they will soon be filled with power from God himself.

Scene four: Bethany

- The disciples go to Bethany, where Jesus blesses them and is 'carried to heaven'. They return to Jerusalem full of delight, and worship God in the Temple.

John

Scene one: the tomb

- Mary Magdalene goes to the tomb before dawn and finds the stone rolled away.

- Mary goes to fetch Peter and John, who come and see for themselves. John begins to understand. They go home!
- Mary, alone, meets Jesus and mistakes him for the gardener. Jesus calls her by name, she recognizes him and wants to hold on to him but is told not to.
- Mary goes back to tell the disciples what has just happened.

Scene two: the upper room

- That evening Jesus appears in the disciples' room, gives them his peace and breathes the Holy Spirit into them.
- Jesus returns the next week, when Thomas is present, and deals directly with Thomas' doubts. Thomas is convinced: 'My Lord and my God!'

Scene three: the lake shore

- Seven of the disciples have returned to Galilee and go fishing with Peter. They catch nothing.
- Jesus appears on the lake shore and enables them to catch a huge haul of fish. Peter recognizes Jesus, puts on some clothes (!) and jumps into the sea.
- Jesus makes them breakfast with bread and fish, no-one daring to ask him the key question, 'Who are you?' They know.
- Jesus restores Peter to his task as a leader with the repeated question, 'Do you love me?' and the command, 'Feed my sheep.'
- Jesus is enigmatic about the future of 'the disciple whom Jesus loved'.

For the full accounts, see all four gospel passages in Appendix 1.

So here we have four accounts of a spectacular series of events. One of the best things to do is simply to become familiar with the different narratives, to enjoy them and relish the different emphases. It's not surprising that there are differences; there would be variations in the reporting of any major event, let alone one which had turned the witnesses' world upside down! But what is also so striking is the unanimity of the accounts on the fundamentals.

- It was first light on Sunday morning.
- The tomb was empty.
- It was the women who were the first witnesses.
- The disciples repeatedly met Jesus.
- His body was the same, but different.
- The disciples only gradually internalized the event.
- The appearances came to a decisive end.
- The disciples were left with a commission.

These four accounts are the raw materials on which people have pondered and prayed for two thousand years. For millions of people they hold the key to an entire way of life and to a new way of understanding the world.

'Have I got news for you?'

Yes!

For further detailed study see the resources section at the end of the book, particularly N. T. Wright, The Resurrection of the Son of God, *SPCK, 2003.*

For reflection 1

The fifth ace

Imagine you're playing a game of poker, late at night. The lights are low, the stakes are high, and you're concentrating like mad. Opposite you is just one player and he's pretty focused too. You put down a royal flush; that should do it. He hesitates. And then with a flourish he puts down five aces. You look at him in disbelief; he looks at you, straight-faced. And then his eyes begin to twinkle, his shoulders begin to heave, and from deep within there emerges the most wonderful, infectious laughter! In a moment, you find yourself caught up in this eruption of absurd joy. The barriers are down. You've lost – and won – at the same time.

The evocative image of God's fifth ace comes from a poem by Anne Sexton,[1] and it seems to me it applies nowhere better than to the resurrection. When everything looked utterly desperate and bleak, when the worst thing in the history of the world had just happened – the Son of God had been killed – God played his fifth ace. His opponents had played their strongest hand; their dark royal flush had been laid on the table; there looked to be no way back. And God trumped the lot.

You could cry 'Unfair!' But who said anything about fairness? Nothing about the cross was fair. The iron savagery of humankind had seen to that. The only way out of this end-of-the-world situation was to make a new one. So God played his fifth ace – the resurrection, the foundational moment of a new creation.

And what can you do with such a wild, unexpected, off-limits initiative? You can only laugh at the reckless absurdity of it. God broke the rules – perhaps for the only time. Or was it that he rewrote the rules to include a previously unthought-of range of possibilities? With the playing of that fifth ace, heaven and earth exploded in laughter and joy, and we're caught up in the divine comedy.

Countless people have found that when they've seemed locked away in a dark corner of life, God has played his fifth ace and the deep

---

[1] From 'The Rowing Endeth', *The Complete Poems*, Houghton Mifflin Company, 1982.

chuckle of resurrection has begun to rise up within them. God doesn't leave us languishing alone in our griefs and sorrows; he's always looking for cracks in the hard ground where green shoots of hope can squeeze through. If God's love is unconditional and irrepressible then that's what you'd expect. But each time it happens it comes with the freshness of miracle – the unexpected shock of a fifth ace.

What actually happened on Easter morning?

It's the basic question. If Jesus wasn't raised that spring morning in Jerusalem then the rest of this book is a bit of a let-down. Or, as Paul put it: 'If Christ has not been raised, your faith is futile!' (1 Cor. 15.17).

We are, however, in disputed territory. Arguments rage in scholarly debate; many people have their own pet theories; many others simply pass it by as unbelievable. So are we dealing with the resurrection of a transformed body or are we dealing with benign self-deception? If we look at the issue head on, biological science will tell us with proper conviction that dead men don't rise, and that has to be our starting point. But immediately we also need to say that we mustn't bring our pre-existing answers to new questions. Let the evidence be looked at.

The challenges

In their search for alternative explanations of this central core of Christian belief, people have come up with a number of challenges. Let's name them:

1 Jesus didn't really die on the cross; he swooned, and later reappeared to revitalize his disciples. In its advanced form this explanation has Jesus marrying Mary Magdalene and going off to live in France.
2 The women went to the wrong tomb. They were distraught because of the task they had to perform, and they got there in the half-light of dawn. Consequently they found another tomb by mistake.
3 The tomb was only empty because Jesus' body had been removed by person or persons unknown – the disciples, the Jewish authorities and the Romans being the chief suspects. Then the whole thing got out of hand with people claiming Jesus had risen from the dead.

4 The appearances of Jesus to his disciples were actually hallucinations produced by the fevered disappointment of the disciples. This often happens to bereaved people, but here the disciples objectified the hallucinations because they were so crippled by the scale of their loss.
5 The stories of resurrection developed as the disciples came to realize that they had a new sense of the continuing presence of Jesus and the importance of his message. They felt loved, forgiven and empowered by the memory and spirit of Jesus, and from that resurgence of confidence they were able to go out and tell the world about his 'risen' life.
6 A variation on the above is that the stories of resurrection actually developed some years after the 'events', to legitimate or defend an idea of resurrection that had grown up, not from what happened that morning in Jerusalem, but from a combination of spiritual experience, new found faith and reflection on the scriptures.
7 A more radical challenge is found in books such as *The Da Vinci Code*, which suggests that the entire resurrection story was inserted much later. The original Christian writings told only of a human Jesus, but Constantine commissioned and financed a new Bible in 325 to make Jesus godlike. The Gospels were then rewritten, but some of the original Christian writings exist in the source document 'Q', in the Dead Sea scrolls and in the Nag Hammadi documents.

Those are some of the main alternatives to the way mainstream Christianity has understood the resurrection event through the centuries. Let's put them to the test.

The background

What was the religious and cultural background out of which the story of Jesus' resurrection emerged? It's clear that there was a Jewish belief in resurrection at the time of Jesus. Not everyone held it – the Sadducees being a prime example (Mark 12.18–27) – but within the spectrum of beliefs about resurrection the clear consensus was that they were talking about *a final physical resurrection at the end of time*, an event for the 'just' on 'the last day'.

What was so revolutionary about the first Christians' claim concerning the resurrection of Jesus is that they were saying that what God was expected to do for all his faithful people at the end of history, he had now done for one man *within* history. Look at the striking ways that Jewish belief in resurrection was reframed by the first Christians:

- Whereas resurrection was a significant belief in Judaism, it was clearly the centrepiece in Christianity.
- Whereas resurrection occupied one point on a spectrum of Jewish belief about God's final purposes, it was the only option in Christianity.
- Whereas Jewish thought saw resurrection as a single event at the very end of time, Christians said it was a two-stage event: Jesus first, then us.
- Whereas in Judaism no-one believed that the Messiah would be raised from the dead (he was a religious/military figure who would restore Israel's fortunes), Christianity claimed that this was fundamental. The resurrection demonstrated that Jesus was indeed the Messiah.

From this we can see that the resurrection of Jesus came out of the blue as far as the religious and cultural background of first-century Palestine was concerned. So the question is, why was it so different? What had happened?

The evidence

No-one saw the resurrection happen. We have no eye-witness accounts of the resurrection itself, and interestingly, no-one at the time tried to make one up. What we have to do is to piece together the available strands of evidence and make the best possible deductions from all the data. There are five main groups of data, although the first two – the empty tomb and the appearances – are the most significant. Let's look at them.

The empty tomb

The clear statement of all four Gospel accounts is that the tomb was empty. There can be no dispute about that basic conviction, but the question we have to tussle with is 'Why?' Is there a better theory to fit the facts?

1 It's very noticeable that the accounts of the resurrection are practically devoid of biblical references or echoes. That's very different from the accounts of the crucifixion, where the biblical allusions from Isaiah and elsewhere are constantly woven into the text. The resurrection stories have a breathless, urgent and dramatic quality, with all the characteristics of eye-witness accounts which have often been repeated.

2 The newscasters, incredibly, are women! The people entrusted with this amazing good news are precisely those in society least likely to be believed. Women in the ancient world were simply not regarded as credible witnesses. Why on earth give the leading testimony to women if the narrative was in any sense contrived? It would be a classic example of shooting yourself in the foot.

3 Furthermore, there is no evidence of the narratives being 'fixed'. Conflicts in the various accounts are more likely to be marks of truthfulness than of unreliability. If the accounts were more uniform you would suspect a single source, whether reliable or not. The presence of variations on the common theme suggests multiple sources and therefore greater reliability. Those four observers of the football match (see 'Have I got news for you!, p. 10) were all sitting in different places!

4 It's worth noting that nobody at the time seems to have disputed the fact of the empty tomb. The only rumour of an alternative explanation is the conspiracy to say that the disciples had stolen the body (Matt. 28.11–15), but even the Jewish leaders don't have an argument with the fact that the tomb was empty.

5 Another interesting sidelight is that there is no evidence in early Christianity of any veneration of the tomb of Jesus. The practice of

veneration at the tomb of a prophet or holy figure was commonplace – as it is today at the tombs of, for example, Abraham or David, or indeed, St Francis, St Cuthbert or any number of saints. Today, of course, huge numbers of Christians are drawn to venerate the tomb of Jesus in the Church of the Holy Sepulchre, but for the first four centuries of Christian history there is no evidence of it at all, nor even of Christians gathering there to worship. They were too busy meeting the risen Lord everywhere else!

6 What are the alternative reasons for the tomb being empty?
   (a) *The disciples moved the body* You would have to say, however, that nothing in the disciples' character would indicate that such a deceit was likely. Moreover, for them to persist in this hoax to the point of martyrdom would be unbelievable. They were not playing silly games.
   (b) *The Jewish leaders moved the body* Matthew indicates that they feared others might do so, not that they had done so themselves. Moreover, if they had taken the body elsewhere they had only to produce it again when these annoying Christians started to claim their Jesus had been raised from the dead. There's nothing like a dead body to quash a rumour of resurrection!
   (c) *The Romans moved the body* Presumably to stop the tomb becoming a place of pilgrimage and insurrection. But again, why not produce the body when things started getting lively? These are some of the answers to Challenge 3 (p. 18).

7 Of course, Challenge 2 suggests simply that the women had gone to the wrong tomb, confused by grief and semi-darkness. But the morning light would soon have dealt with that problem. Less confused people – disciples, guards, Jewish leaders – would soon have gone to the proper tomb and stopped that silly rumour.

8 There remains the theory that Jesus had only swooned on the cross and not actually died. This must be the most fanciful of the alternatives people sometimes suggest. This man had been flogged almost to death, then crucified by experienced executioners, had a spear thrust into his side to make sure of death, been placed in a tomb

behind a massive stone, and left for 48 hours without any medical attention. It simply isn't conceivable that he should then have recovered so well that he could roll back that stone by himself and emerge so full of health and vitality that he could convince his followers that he was the conqueror of death, the Prince of Life. This is an answer to Challenge 1 (p. 18). With regard to the developed version of this story, that Jesus married Mary Magdalene and went off to live in Western Europe, it has to be pointed out that there is no credible historical evidence that would detain a serious academic historian beyond the pages of fiction. We have to apply the same standards of scholarly rigour to fanciful conspiracy theories as we do to conventional historical research.

So our consideration of the empty tomb points us pretty conclusively to the factual truth of the claim. However, that does not prove that the resurrection occurred. All it proves is that there was an empty tomb, for whatever reason (although some reasons are less credible than others). In other words, the empty tomb is a *necessary* fact for the resurrection story to be true, but it's not in itself a *sufficient* fact. We need more.

The resurrection appearances

Our quick overview of the resurrection narratives ('Have I got news for you!' pp. 11–15) demonstrates how many different appearances of the risen Jesus are recorded in the Gospels. He was seen at the tomb, in the upper room (on at least two occasions), on an evening walk back to Emmaus, by the sea shore in Galilee, and on a mountain top, among other places. He appeared to Mary Magdalene, to Peter, to James, to the disciples several times, to 'more than five hundred brothers and sisters at one time' (1 Cor. 15.6). All this needs to be assessed. Was it imagination, hallucination, wish-fulfilment? What do we make of it?

1 We need to be clear that we are into very early testimony here. Paul wrote his first letter to the Corinthians in the early 50s, no more than twenty-five years after Jesus died. There would have been many eye-witnesses who could have corroborated or disproved the claim that five hundred people saw him at one time, 'most of whom', Paul

is careful to point out, 'are still alive.' 'Go and ask them yourselves!' is what Paul is saying. Moreover Paul was converted only two or three years after Jesus' death and he clearly had his initial instruction as a Christian very soon after that, so the testimony in 1 Corinthians 15.3–8 goes back to within two or three years of the events themselves.

2 The descriptions of the appearances are again very fresh and uncontrived. They have about them the ring of truth. There's no attempt to provide a coherent sequence of events, and their very randomness is supportive of their authenticity. Here again we see testimony being entrusted to women. Interestingly, we can see in 1 Corinthians 15.3–8 how the women are already beginning to be screened out in the first 'official' account of what happened. Their experience of meeting Jesus isn't recorded, but somehow an appearance to James has crept in! There are many other little clues to the genuineness of these accounts. How about Matthew's little aside in 28.17: 'When they saw him they worshipped him; *but some doubted*.' This doubt isn't shown as being resolved, so it's not an artificial device to show how our doubts too can be overcome. It looks like the observation of an eye-witness.

3 Let's be clear: no-one was expecting to see Jesus after his death. Jewish believers had no expectation of an individual resurrection; they envisaged only a final resurrection of all the faithful at the last day. The appearance of Jesus would have been an utter surprise and could not be put down to wish-fulfilment. This is one of the answers to Challenge 4.

4 We also need to reckon with the sheer diversity of the appearances over such an extended period. These were not simple people. They were used to dreams, certainly, but they knew the difference between a dream and a real appearance. Moreover, there are many reports in contemporary literature of the period of visions of ancient heroes of the faith, such as Abel and Jeremiah and the mysterious figure in Daniel. But in these visions the figure is seen as robed in heavenly glory, a figure of majesty. In the case of Jesus we're dealing with someone they had been with just a few days previously,

and he's not now seen in any of the trappings of conventional apocalyptic. It's just Jesus. Most important of all, in none of these other cases was there a hint that those who saw the visions concluded that these people had been raised from the dead. That idea was utterly unique. In other words, the appearances of Jesus were completely unlike the dreams and visions of contemporary culture. This is another of the answers to Challenge 4.

5 Paul has sometimes been cited as being an exception to the normal 'sightings' of Jesus, and therefore encouraging a more vision-like understanding of the risen Christ. After all, he puts himself in the line of those to whom Jesus appeared after the resurrection, even though it was some time after those appearances had come to an end with the ascension. 'Last of all, as to one untimely born, he appeared also to me' (1 Cor. 15.8). Paul is clear that it's the same Jesus who appeared to him as to the other disciples, but equally that it was a different type of appearance – note the blinding light, the heavenly voice, the falling to the ground (Acts 9.1–9), quite unlike the other appearances. And yet Paul is clearly speaking of a bodily resurrection in 1 Corinthians 15.3–4, where he maintains that he is handing on what he has received, 'that he was buried, and that he was raised on the third day'. These are parallel physical events: burial and being raised. So, as he says, 'If Christ has not been raised, your faith is futile' (v. 17). And remember, Paul was brought up as a Pharisee; he would have understood resurrection in purely physical terms, not as a spiritual vision.

6 Of course, where the accounts of the appearances really struggle is in describing what the resurrection body of Jesus was like. All the Gospel writers can do is record what they knew or what the tradition clearly said. So we have a resurrection body that at certain times is decidedly physical, as in Luke, where Jesus says, 'Touch me and see, for a ghost does not have flesh and bones as you see that I have' (Luke 24.39). At other times, Jesus' body simply appears and disappears at will. Paul writes of a future 'spiritual body' (1 Cor. 15.44), although this has often been misunderstood: Paul did not mean by this 'a person made of spirit', as if that person would be

> ghostly and vacuous, but rather 'a new body animated by God's Spirit', robust and full of life. So Jesus' risen body might perhaps be described as having a 'transformed physicality', neither a resuscitated body nor a thing of pure spirit. This may sound strange, but we're in the realm here of a new creation, the anticipation in time of what God intends for the whole of his world at the end of time. (And in any case, doesn't carbon, for example, exist sometimes as graphite and sometimes as diamond, the one soft and flaky, the other hard and crystalline? Doesn't H_2O exist sometimes as water, sometimes as ice and sometimes as steam? If this kind of variation in the *form* of the same atoms can co-exist in this current created order, how much more could it be so in a new creation?)

These considerations about the appearances of Jesus have led most Christians to conclude that Jesus was indeed encountered by very many different people over an extended period of time, but that after a few weeks those appearances suddenly stopped. The resurrection appearances were a gift so that we could truly know that death was defeated.

We now have another piece of evidence that turns out to be *necessary* if Jesus is to be risen, but is still not *sufficient* of itself. There could be other reasons why people saw Jesus in these ways (although they turn out to be relatively unconvincing). But when you put together the two major pieces of evidence – the empty tomb and the appearances – you come to a conclusion that seems both necessary *and* sufficient – that this Jesus was indeed risen from the dead.

The transformation of the disciples

We're looking at the evidence. We've considered the two major factors but there are others. Take the fact that the disciples were stopped in their tracks, turned around, and sent off in a completely different direction. We have a most remarkable picture of the 'before' and 'after' of this band of brothers. Before whatever happened, they were broken and demoralized. They had denied or deserted Jesus, almost to a man. They were hiding away for fear of capture and being treated in the same way as Jesus. They had hoped that he was the one to rescue Israel (Luke 24.21) but they'd been mistaken.

Compare this with the picture of those same people we encounter in the early chapters of Acts, where fearlessly and joyfully they go around telling everyone what they've seen and heard. They're arrested, harassed, threatened, beaten up, martyred, but they're unstoppable. Something radical has happened. They're different men. Would they die for a lie or a mistake? Moreover, would they be so fundamentally transformed if they thought the resurrection really only amounted to 'a new sense of the continuing presence of Jesus and the importance of his message'? It hardly seems likely. By 'resurrection' they clearly meant that something had happened to Jesus himself, not that something had only happened to *them.* This is one of the answers to Challenges 5 and 6.

The existence and growth of the Church

This carries on from the point above. The early Church was soon exploding in size. We get some picture of that growth from the description of 3,000 people wanting to be baptized after Peter's Pentecost sermon, recorded in Acts 2. Within a hundred years most Christians seemed to be coming from the Gentile world, and within three hundred years the might of Rome had fallen to the carpenter from Galilee. So it has gone on, until today almost one third of the world's population, some 2,000 million people worldwide, claim to be followers of Jesus. That's an enormous edifice to be based on a lie or a mistake. It's hard to imagine how the Church could have such range and influence without it being founded on events and experiences that are fundamentally factual and true. Feeling 'loved, forgiven and empowered by the memory and spirit of Jesus' hardly seems sufficient to sustain such an extraordinary growth in the Church over two millennia. This is also one of the answers to Challenges 5 and 6.

The high estimation of Jesus

There is a truly amazing story to tell here. Within a few years of Jesus' death the first Christians – including many who had known him in the flesh – were speaking about him in divine terms. They were calling him 'Lord'. Indeed, Paul calls Jesus 'Lord' all the time. Now 'Lord' was the way that Greek-speaking Jews referred to God himself, and Jews were fiercely monotheistic, absolutely resolute that God is one, and beside him there is no other. Yet here they were calling Jesus 'Lord', the man they'd known as a carpenter from Nazareth, who they'd chatted and joked with on the road, who they'd seen get tired and hungry, and sometimes overwhelmed. This was the man they had seen with their own eyes, looked at and touched with their own hands (1 John 1.1). To call him 'Lord' was a remarkable leap of imagination and recognition.

If we're in any doubt about how serious this claim was, we can simply look at Philippians 2.5–11:

> Jesus, who, though he was in the form of God, did not regard equality with God as something to be exploited, but emptied himself, taking the form of a slave . . . Therefore God . . . gave him the name that is above every name, so that at the name of Jesus every knee should bend, in heaven and on earth and under the earth, and every tongue should confess that Jesus Christ is Lord.

This is staggering material to emerge from a Jewish background within twenty or so years of a human life and death. It needs something of massive importance to have happened. Again, the idea that the disciples had simply realized that the teaching and significance of Jesus could not die hardly seems sufficient to sustain and explain this enormous claim to Jesus' divinity. Only a fully risen Christ will do it. This is another part of the answer to Challenges 5 and 6.

The results of good scholarship

We need to address finally Challenge 7, the conspiracy theory of books such as *The Da Vinci Code*, which maintain that the earliest Christian records contained no divine status for Jesus, and certainly no resurrection. These, they say, were added in the fourth century by Constantine, eager to bolster the power of the Church. This wild thesis finds no support in any respectable academic circles. Each of the documents quoted in *The Da Vinci Code* – 'Q', the Dead Sea scrolls and the Nag Hammadi documents – have been known about for decades. 'Q' is already known to be a major source in the 'synoptic' Gospels. The Dead Sea scrolls say nothing about Jesus. They are very valuable to scholars in giving background information about the New Testament world but they make no claim to be Christian at all. And the Nag Hammadi documents were gnostic material, nearly all written much later than the Gospels, and with very little narrative about Jesus. All this material is well known to scholars and is in no way 'secret knowledge' which the Church has been repressing. The material merely provides interesting insights about contemporary religious beliefs. No scholar, Christian or otherwise, would give a moment's credence to the fanciful and, in the end, absurd claims of the conspiracy theories of Challenge 7. They wouldn't be worth mentioning except that so many people seem to have been taken in by the myths of a very good story-teller.

A provisional conclusion

How can it be anything but provisional? We're dealing here with things that defy the wit and intelligence of mere humans to understand. We're moving far beyond the ordinary categories of empirical research and rationality. But that is inevitable if this event is to be what Christians have always claimed it to be. The resurrection of Jesus is the first-fruits of the new creation that God intends at the end of time; it's the hors d'oeuvre of the heavenly banquet. Alternative explanations that require less intellectual humility may be attractive but they're not ultimately convincing. To say that Jesus is alive in a purely spiritual sense and that we give him and his teachings our allegiance, is simply not up to the task.

The conclusion of international scholar Tom Wright is to the point:

> We are left with the secure historical conclusion: the tomb was empty, and various meetings took place not only between Jesus and his followers but also between Jesus and people who had not been among his followers. I regard this conclusion as coming in the same sort of category – of historical probability so high as to be virtually certain – as the death of Augustus in AD 14 or the fall of Jerusalem in AD 70.[2]

And you can't say fairer than that!

---

[2] N. T. Wright, *The Resurrection of the Son of God*, SPCK, 2003, p. 710.

For reflection 2

The feast of the unexpected

Some things just keep on coming round, like taxes, the Queen's Christmas message and the defeat of the England football team in a penalty shoot-out. These are things we can anticipate and prepare for with a sense of inevitability.

There's a danger that we might treat the resurrection of Christ in the same way. After all, it comes round each year. So we might begin to take this most breath-taking event for granted ('Oh, it's just Jesus rising from the dead again!').

But Easter isn't like the inevitable return of spring, the endless cycle of the seasons. Easter is about the cataclysmic shattering of the tomb of death. It's the breaking in of a new world. It's what J. R. R. Tolkien called 'a joy beyond the walls of the world'.

So woe betide us if we try to domesticate this extraordinary drama and turn it into a conventional happy ending. Easter is the feast of the unexpected. No-one can say, 'I told you so!' about Easter. It isn't that kind of experience. It's utterly new and it ought to break open the concrete walls of our thinking each time it happens.

Through the rest of the year we tend to return to default mode in which events are cyclical and time is circular. By contrast, resurrection time is vertical. It crashes in from above and breaks open our religious domesticity. Men and women have always wanted to gain control over their lives. They want to be able to weigh life, measure it out, remove the surprise – anything to emasculate the gods.

But Christ arrives from death without warning and without permission. He disturbs every attempt to make God predictable and religion safe. To some this is what they'd always feared: God would get out of the box and cause untold trouble.

To others, this is the intoxication of true faith – the feast of the unexpected and the birth of a new world.

What happened next?

WHAT THE DISCIPLES DID AFTER THE RESURRECTION

The disciples were transformed by the experience of the resurrection, and after an initial time together in Jerusalem and Galilee they moved off in all directions to take the good news of Jesus to all parts of the known world. However, apart from Peter's story and one or two others, we tend to get a bit sketchy over the details of most of the disciples, and in any case, the stories easily slip over into legend. But if we are to try and 'live Easter through the year' it can be helpful to mark the saints' days in the Church's calendar and remember the astonishing travels of these brave men.

First of all, a reminder of who they were:

> Then Jesus summoned his twelve disciples and gave them authority . . . These are the names of the twelve apostles: first Simon, also known as Peter, and his brother Andrew; James son of Zebedee, and his brother John; Philip and Bartholomew; Thomas and Matthew the tax collector; James son of Alphaeus, and Thaddaeus; Simon the Cananaean, and Judas Iscariot, the one who betrayed him. (Matt. 10.1–4)

3 May: Philip

Philip was from Bethsaida and was the one who persuaded Nathanael to come and see Jesus. At the feeding of the 5,000 he was sceptical that the food would go round, and he also appears in John's Gospel asking Jesus to 'show us the Father'. His subsequent history is obscure. He has been connected with 'Asia' and it's reported that he died of natural causes in Hierapolis. Other traditions describe him as having been crucified, so that his symbol (at other times loaves, from the feeding of the 5,000) is a tall cross. This is not the same Philip who was chosen in

Acts 6 to serve the needy and then had the fascinating encounter with the Ethiopian eunuch on the road to Gaza in Acts 8.

3 May: James the Less

James has the nickname 'the Less' simply because he was younger than James 'the Great'. It has been claimed that he became head of the church in Jerusalem and was put to death by the Sanhedrin in AD 62. However, it appears that the head of that church was 'James the Lord's brother' (Gal. 1.19), and not 'James son of Alphaeus'. In which case, we know nothing more of him!

29 June: Peter

This most famous of the apostles was the headstrong fisherman on whom Jesus said he would build his Church. After the ascension Peter takes the lead in the young Church, speaking on the day of Pentecost (Acts 2.14–36), performing the first miracle (Acts 3.1–9), speaking when he and John are brought before the Sanhedrin (Acts 4.1–21), opening the Church to the Gentiles by admitting Cornelius (Acts 10.1–11), and speaking powerfully at the Council of Jerusalem (Acts 15). He went to Rome and shared authority with Paul for the church there. The famous 'Quo Vadis' legend has Peter running away from Rome when he meets Jesus carrying his cross and walking back to the city. 'Where are you going?' says Peter. 'Back to Rome to be crucified afresh,' says Jesus. Peter gets the message and returns! The historian Eusebius quotes Origen as saying that Peter was crucified head down, at his request, not being worthy of the same death as his Lord. This was probably in AD 64 in the persecutions of Nero. A later tradition of Jerome that he was bishop of Rome for twenty-five years before his martyrdom is less well supported. It is quite likely that the tomb below the altar in St Peter's, Rome, is in fact his resting place.

3 July: Thomas

Thomas, 'the twin', is known to the Christian world as the disciple who doubted the resurrection but who later came out with the first explicit affirmation of Jesus' divinity, 'My Lord and my God' (John 20.28). The apocryphal Acts of Thomas credit him with taking the gospel to India and describe his missionary activities there in thirteen long sections. The Syrian Christians of Malabar call themselves 'Christians of St Thomas' and are clear that they were evangelized by Thomas, who was martyred and buried at Mylapore near Madras. The sixth-century Thomas Cross speaks of him lying there, although his remains are said to have travelled via Edessa in the fourth century to their current resting place in Ortona, Italy.

25 July: James the Great

The son of Zebedee and brother of John. These 'sons of thunder' were part of the inner group who, with Peter, were taken into Jesus' closest confidence on the Mount of Transfiguration and in the Garden of Gethsemane. James was the first of the apostles to be martyred, being beheaded by Herod Agrippa in AD 44 (Acts 12.2). The tradition of the early Church is that the apostles did not leave Jerusalem until after James' death, which makes it highly unlikely that the seventh-century tradition that James took the gospel to Spain is authentic. Nevertheless, from the ninth century there has been a tradition that the body of James was taken to Santiago de Compostela, and in the Middle Ages James was one of the most popular saints in Spain.

24 August: Bartholomew

Bartholomew is only mentioned in the Gospels in the various lists of disciples, but his name actually means only 'son of Tolmai'; it may be that he had another personal name, possibly Nathanael, in which case he is the one Jesus identified as 'an Israelite in whom there is no deceit' (John 1.47). According to the historian bishop Eusebius, a teacher called Pantaenus was visiting India between AD 150 and 200, and he found the Gospel of Matthew left behind by 'Bartholomew, one of the Apostles'. Had Bartholomew reached India? We don't know, but Bartholomew's sad end was to be flayed alive in Armenia. He was then beheaded, and his emblem in religious art is a butcher's knife.

His relics are said eventually to have been taken back to Benevento in Italy.

21 September: Matthew

Matthew was the tax collector for the Romans in Capernaum whose life was turned around by an encounter with Jesus recorded in Matthew 9.9. The Gospel under his name may not have been written by Matthew himself, even though his name has been attached to it since the second century, but Matthew may have provided the material not found in Mark. Little is known of Matthew's later life. Eusebius says he preached to the Hebrews – which doesn't take us much further forward. Some traditions place his martyrdom in Ethiopia, and in later times Salerno has been among the places to claim his relics. Christian symbolism has usually given Matthew the form simply of a man, on the grounds that the genealogy in Matthew's Gospel demonstrates Jesus' human origin. In religious art he is likely to be depicted with a sword, a money-bag or a carpenter's square.

28 October: Simon

The designation 'the Cananaean' is probably a transcription of the Aramaic word for 'zealous'. That could apply to the quality of his commitment or to his being a member of the Zealot party, which was dedicated to ejecting the Romans from the land. One tradition describes the preaching and martyrdom of Simon and Jude together in Persia. See how these apostles got around!

28 October: Jude

Jude is 'Judas son of James' in Luke 6, 'Judas (not Iscariot)' in John 14, and probably Thaddaeus in Matthew 10 and Mark 3. In the West he has generally been taken to be not 'son of James' but 'brother of James' in Jude 1, one of Jesus' brothers (identified as James, Joses, Simon and Judas in Mark 6.3). So here he is, a brother of Jesus, writer of the epistle, and close colleague of Simon. And sadly he came to the same end as his friend in Persia.

30 November: Andrew

Andrew was the brother of Peter but not one of the inner group of three disciples. Not much is known of his later life except that he preached the gospel in Scythia, but, as ever, there are traditions associated with his death. This is supposed to have taken place in Patras, in present-day Greece, in AD 60, when Andrew was crucified on a cross in the shape of an X. He has been the patron saint of Scotland since about 750 and also holds that honour in Greece and Russia. Because of him bringing his brother Peter to meet Jesus, Andrew is regarded as the first Christian missionary, and prayers for mission are often focused around St Andrew's Day.

27 December: John

With Peter and James, John was one of the inner group of disciples around Jesus. He crops up many times in the Gospels, with the traditional assumption being that he was 'the disciple who Jesus loved' in John's Gospel. He was therefore the one who was close to Jesus at the Last Supper, was entrusted at the cross with looking after Jesus' mother, ran with Peter to the tomb on Easter morning and recognized the risen Lord by the sea shore. Tradition has credited John with a Gospel, three letters and the book of Revelation, but these attributions are disputed, often with preference going to a 'school' of the beloved disciple. Again, tradition has it that John eventually settled in Ephesus with Mary the mother of Jesus, after an active ministry with Peter recorded in the early chapters of Acts. One fairly unreliable story has John martyred with James in AD 44, while another legend has John ordered by the persecuting Emperor Domitian to be thrown into a cauldron of boiling oil 'before the Latin gate' in Rome, an experience from which he is supposed to have emerged unharmed. Who knows? But John is a considerable figure in Christian thought and memory.

And that leaves just one of the twelve who has no date of commemoration because he did the unforgivable – he betrayed his Lord.

Judas Iscariot

This sad figure has borne the wrath of the Christian world ever since the dark events of the night of the Last Supper. As John records it, 'He immediately went out. And it was night' (John 13.30). Matthew clearly records his subsequent death as suicide when he realized that he had betrayed innocent blood (Matt. 27.4), although this is the only reference to his death being at his own hands. Whatever the darkness and confusion that took over Judas' mind, he has been regarded with abhorrence ever since. Perhaps there is need for a note of hope, as is beautifully suggested in the following poem by Ruth Etchells.

Ballad of the Judas Tree

In Hell there grew a Judas Tree
Where Judas hanged and died
Because he could not bear to see
His master crucified

Our Lord descended into Hell
And found his Judas there
For ever hanging on the tree
Grown from his own despair

So Jesus cut his Judas down
And took him in his arms
'It was for this I came' he said
'And not to do you harm.

'My Father gave me twelve good men
And all of them I kept
Though one betrayed and one denied
Some fled and others slept.

'In three days' time I must return
To make the others glad
But first I had to come to Hell
And share the death you had.

‘My tree will grow in place of yours
Its roots strike here as well.
There is no final victory
Without this soul from Hell.’

So when we all condemn him
As of every traitor worst
Remember that of all his men
Our Lord forgave him first.

For reflection 3

The Gardener

In John's account of the first Easter morning Mary Magdalene turns around from the now-empty tomb (empty, that is, apart from a couple of characters in white!), and bumps into a man she takes to be the gardener. They have this wonderful conversation where Mary asks him to tell her where the body of her best friend has been taken, and he simply says her name, in the way that only special friends do. 'Mary!' he says. 'Teacher!' she answers, with all the emotion that means 'My own teacher! My own special friend!'

But first of all Mary thinks Jesus is the gardener. How wrong could she be – and yet, how right! The irony is that he *is* in fact the

'And then he said: "I need your clothes . . ."'

gardener – the Gardener of the new Creation that has gloriously begun that morning. God hasn't just polished up the old creation, tired and careworn as it was. That garden had become terribly overgrown with thickets of obscure religious practices and weeds of injustice and oppression that seemed utterly resistant to sensible husbandry. What God had done this happy morning was to start again. 'In the beginning God created . . .' (Genesis 1). 'In the beginning was the Word . . .' (John 1). And here was the new Adam in the new Garden. Creation was beginning again.

That's why belief in the resurrection is such an explosive force in the world. No part of human existence is unaffected by a new Creation. The worlds of politics, the arts, science and technology, economics, the legal system, the way we handle international conflict and the way we look after the first creation – everything is brought into the orbit of the risen Christ, the second Adam in the new garden. Through this we anticipate the final renewal of creation – the new heaven and the new earth (Revelation 21, 22).

Moreover, at the personal level we can experience now what's in store for the whole of creation eventually – a life brought into joyful partnership with the risen, ascended Christ. That's what the risen life of the Christian is meant to be. We probably think to ourselves, 'I wish . . . !' We know only too well what it's like to struggle with the 'old creation' still deeply embedded within us. We know the struggles and failures, the weariness and loss of vision. But maybe we haven't yet glimpsed how radical this new creation really can be. 'If anyone is in Christ there is a new creation. Everything old has passed away; see, everything has become new' (2 Cor. 5.17). That sounds like a promise to write on our hearts.

For further information, contact the Gardener.

If it's true

THE IMPLICATIONS

In the section 'What actually happened on Easter morning?' (pp. 18–30) I argued for the truth of the resurrection as recorded in the Gospels. But this isn't one of those truths you can simply file away under 'R'. The implications are enormous. We each have to make up our own minds, but if it's true . . .

If it's true, Jesus is vindicated

We can have confidence that what he said and did was authenticated by God. The things he said were indeed the closest we can get to the mind of God, and the things he did were assuredly owned by God and were clear imprints of the Father's will. Jesus was no maverick messiah in the line of many other fraudulent claimants. He truly was God's self-portrait, God's Son.

If it's true, evil has been disarmed

The reign of evil has had a long and dishonourable history. It was unleashed on Jesus in total warfare on that demonic cross. Here were focused the hatred, cruelty and violence of human behaviour, the lust for power, the selfishness of individuals and the compromise of groups, the arrogance and vanity of humankind, the shoddiness of religion, and so much more. Jesus took all of this without flinching. He absorbed it without reproach. He returned love for hate, forgiveness for cruelty. And in so doing he disarmed the powers at their strongest point. There was nothing more they could do in the face of such love. Except quit the field.

If it's true, the iron gates of death have been broken open

The last enemy is death. It's the great leveller, the vast uncertainty, 'the dark wind blowing from the future' (Camus). Woody Allen spoke for many: 'It's not that I'm afraid to die. I just don't want to be there when it happens.' Fear of death, the process of dying and the meeting of judgement beyond, has dominated ordinary people's religious thinking for thousands of years. But in the resurrection we find that Jesus has broken open those forbidding gates and a joyful light floods into our world. Death isn't the gateway to a world of judgement and shadows but to a God whose mercy is unending. We can joyously abandon life and go into God's good future. Death isn't the end; there is glorious life beyond. The resurrection marks the abolition of death. It's the day death died. And what is promised ultimately is nothing less than a new heaven and a new earth – with Jesus at the centre.

If it's true, life has a framework and a meaning beyond itself

If we live and work within the closed borders of a godless and capricious world it might seem like very good advice to eat, drink and be merry without thought for tomorrow or for anyone else. But something in the human heart always resists this simple recipe for a happy life. We are naturally 'makers of meaning', and believe that life isn't just a disordered, chaotic void and death isn't just the final snuffing out of a pointless life. The resurrection confirms that this instinct is a sure one and that we are set within an eternal context guaranteed by God. The trick then is to live as people who really believe it.

If it's true, Jesus is alive!

However that phrase strikes you, the central affirmation is splendidly unavoidable. By examining the resurrection of Jesus, many people have been forced to the conclusion that if Jesus has been raised from the dead then he has to be alive and accessible today. So there's no reason not to try and get to know him! Through the resurrection Jesus is let loose in the world. The followers of Jesus had found that they could encounter him in a garden, an upper room, on a walk out of town, by a lake, or on a mountain top. Now we find that we can encounter him in our own lives and by our side, in bread and wine, in prayer, in our neighbour and – astonishingly – even in our enemy.

If it's true, we have the offer of a transforming friendship

This follows from the above. If it's true that Jesus is alive then we can have a relationship with him. Not a relationship quite like any other. Jesus often tends to be quieter than we'd like. But a relationship that's sometimes a quiet following and sometimes a demanding discipleship. As we reflect on Jesus' life, death and resurrection it becomes clearer what values and priorities we should live by. As we meet him in communion and prayer we find a different spirit becoming part of our lives. As we meet him in others we find a challenge being placed on our lives which can't be swept aside. This is all part of the transforming friendship offered by the risen Christ.

If it's true, we are right to believe in life in a world obsessed with violence and death

Our global society seems to be intoxicated with violence, and death follows violence in every part of the world. But in his resurrection Jesus says no to this omnivorous power. Believers in the resurrection are given a mandate to promote life in all its fullness, to celebrate life and to encourage an uncompromising love of it. This also implies generosity to others as they seek to enjoy life too. The resurrection subverts the world's terrible reliance on violence as the way to resolve differences. It calls us always to use the strategies of life, not the weapons of death.

If it's true, we can aim high because the sky's not the limit

The resurrection confirms that we're created in God's image and that we're people with astonishing dreams and huge potential. The philosopher Bertrand Russell believed that there was 'no splendour, no vastness anywhere', and when he died there would just be 'triviality for a moment and then nothing'. The resurrection offers another account of human personhood and potential. 'We are children of God, and if children, then heirs, heirs of God and joint heirs with Christ' (Rom. 8.16–17). If it's true, the resurrection of Christ confirms the latter reading. The future looks good!

If it's true, the life of the world – politics, science, the arts and the rest – all matter

Why is that? Because matter matters and has a place in God's future and his purposes. The resurrection of Jesus was a bodily resurrection, not a resuscitation or a merely spiritual resurrection. In other words, the material life of this world mattered to God and was raised in Jesus (with different qualities) as the precursor of the new world he will bring into being in the final act of his new creation. Therefore the world of intellectual thought, of science and technology, of the law, the political system, international relations, economics and development – even the Church – all of this matters to a God who has validated the significance of the material world. Christians therefore are called to enter fully into these pursuits, not as ends in themselves (in that lies idolatry) but as constituent parts of a world loved by God and anticipating a new kingdom of divine abundance.

If it's true, then justice is non-negotiable

This follows on from the last point, but let's be specific. God's clear goal is to put the world to rights – the Bible is shot through with that passion. He started to do it through the death of Jesus and his resurrection from the dead, and he continues to do it through his people as they anticipate, and work for, the just world order of God's new kingdom. So, for example, believers in the resurrection will be committed to the ending of global debt or the elimination of landmines or the survival of our fragile eco-system – not only as ends in themselves but also as essential outworkings of God's good agenda for his whole creation. The resurrection puts us on notice that accepting injustice and the status quo simply isn't acceptable in a world which God intends to be 'put to rights'.

And is it true? For if it is, everything has shifted; the world and everything in it is ready to be transformed

For reflection 4
Odds and ends

I suppose at one level you could say that Jesus' ministry was a matter of odds and ends. He didn't come out with a mission statement, a consultation document or a clearly articulated three-year plan. His PR machine was non-existent, simply relying on word of mouth. His choice of senior managers was eccentric, to say the least.

But more than that, it's difficult to see where the coherence lay in what he did. Maybe there was a rolling programme of teaching and healing but it all seemed to be a bit hit and miss. After all, what did he actually do? He had an encounter here, a conversation there, a healing, a meal, a conversation with the Pharisees. He sailed a bit, took his friends away on retreat once or twice, had the odd holiday with friends in Bethany. He enjoyed barbecues, probably played the occasional game of football on the beach.

But what did it all add up to? Every so often you think you've got a clue. He turns their route deliberately towards Jerusalem or he spells out a bit more about this mysterious thing he calls 'the kingdom of God'. Sometimes you can see the disciples hit a raw nerve, which probably meant they were getting a bit close to the heart of the project. When Peter finds himself called 'Satan', for example, just because he protested at Jesus' facing death; that seemed a bit harsh.

So this whole ministry seems like a collection of fascinating, colourful odds and ends. And the time comes when, for all their beauty, these pieces seem to have been swept up and thrown to the winds, one terrible day in Jerusalem.

But then a strange thing happened and it seemed as if God took all these odds and ends and wove them together into 'a single garment of salvation'. Those bits and pieces of Jesus' life started to fall into place. They began to make sense to those bewildered friends he'd left behind, and they've been making more and more sense ever since. The kaleidoscope of individual actions that made up Jesus' life has assumed patterns of meaning and hope for millions. And the bits and pieces of our lives, which often look so random and without obvious purpose, these minor acts of kindness and generosity, of love and prayer, now assume much greater value. Nothing we try to do well will be lost.

The event that changed everything took place on Easter morning in a garden in Jerusalem. The task of understanding what happened there, and what the implications are, will go on for ever. 'There are also many other things that Jesus did; if every one of them were written down, I suppose that the world itself could not contain the books that would be written' (John 21.25).

Not just odds and ends, but the biography of God.

They said this

The Gospels do not explain the resurrection; the resurrection explains the Gospels. Belief in the resurrection is not an appendage to the Christian faith; it *is* the Christian faith. **John Whale**

[Christ] has forced open a door that has been locked since the death of the first man. He has met, fought and beaten the King of Death. Everything is different because he has done so. **C. S. Lewis**

Jesus' resurrection is the beginning of God's new project, not to snatch people away from earth to heaven, but to colonize earth with the life of heaven. That, after all, is what the Lord's Prayer is about.
Tom Wright

Life is a poor, bare thing without the sap of Christ's resurrection life flowing through it. **Terence Handley MacMath**

In Assisi, in the great basilica, are the bones of St Francis. In Durham, behind the high altar, are the bones of St Cuthbert. But in Jerusalem, under the great rotunda of the Church of the Holy Sepulchre, you find only an empty tomb. **Anon**

Our Lord has written the promise of resurrection, not in books alone, but in every leaf in springtime. **Martin Luther**

In its favour as a living truth there exists such overwhelming evidence, positive and negative, factual and circumstantial, that no intelligent jury in the world could fail to bring in the verdict that the resurrection story is true. **Lord Darling, former Lord Chief Justice**

In Western Europe we have long been preoccupied with sin and death and with what sin and death did to Christ, instead of being preoccupied with Christ, and with what Christ did to sin and death.
Michael Stancliffe

The tomb was empty; death was empty, hell was empty! Jesus was alive. If you ask 'how?', you've missed the joke. Only people who like plastic flowers would indulge in the pedantry of explanation. But when you get it, you will find it hard to keep the smile off your face. **Mike Riddell**

Question to Lesslie Newbigin: 'Are you an optimist or a pessimist?' Answer: 'I'm neither an optimist nor a pessimist. Jesus Christ is risen from the dead.' **Lesslie Newbigin**

No resurrection. No Christianity. **Michael Ramsey**

Part Two

‘WE ARE AN EASTER PEOPLE’
Celebrating the resurrection

Celebrating the Big Day

We know how to let our hair down at Christmas. There are parties and dinners and presents. We decorate our homes, inside and out. We send cards and make phone calls, promising to meet before next Christmas. We plan our TV schedule and empty the supermarket shelves on Christmas Eve. We even let Jesus make a guest appearance.

On Easter Sunday, Wayne picked his way through the mass of pagan symbolism

But what about Easter? Here is the great Christian festival, without which there would be no such thing as 'Christian' anyway. Here is the turning point of history, the hinge on which the destiny of the world swung open. And we don't seem to know what to do with it except see it as a holiday weekend, the first big exodus to the airports.

So here are some ideas on how to raise the stakes. Nothing is adequate to the task of celebrating such an event, but at least we might do better than a few cream eggs and yellow chicks!

- *Egg rolling* Down a hill. The hard-boiled egg that goes furthest without breaking is the winner. Egg rolling symbolizes the breaking open of the tomb.
- *Treasure hunt* In the house or garden for chocolate mini-eggs.
- *Egg painting* A competition to decorate the eggs in the most attractive way.
- *Easter garden* Supply a tray and some raw materials; offer the rest of the garden for further raw materials. Then see what originality emerges.
- *Easter DVD or video* Might be available for children: *The Lion, the Witch and the Wardrobe* would do excellently.
- *Easter lunch or dinner* We have Christmas lunches and dinners, so why not Easter? Lamb should be the meat, or fish, as a reminder of the resurrection meals in Luke 24 and John 21. An empty place can be set for the risen Christ. Grace can take the form of a reading of one of the resurrection meals, and a prayer of thanks.
- *Easter competition* The church could have a creative arts competition on the theme of Easter. The categories could be art, clay modelling, egg painting, photography, poetry, Easter gardens on a tray, spring flower arranging, etc. Age categories could also apply.
- *Home decoration* We decorate our homes with great ingenuity (and expense) at Christmas, so why not at Easter? Yellow and white daffodils are obvious, but how about yellow and white balloons – they can even be attached to car aerials! Or we could use yellow and white streamers, cloths which flow down in our hallway, full of life and light, symbolizing the life flowing out of the empty tomb.

- *Easter presents* Again, why should Christmas have all the good moments? The giving of gifts could be a lovely sign of the gift of new life in the risen Christ. Easter gifts should be more measured than the profligate Christmas extravagances. In particular, they might be more symbolic of beauty, grace and simplicity – those hallmarks of the resurrection. Flowers, music CDs, simple foods, pottery or articles of beauty, life-affirming books – these are the things that enhance a life and speak of a graceful God.
- *Easter surprises* Nothing catches us out more than receiving something totally unexpected and unearned. We're not used to getting 'something for nothing'. So it can be a wonderful sign of the sheer grace of God in the resurrection when we do something radically generous. Some churches take a gift of flowers to the houses around about, 'With love from God/the Church' (depending on taste). Some Americans (wouldn't you know it?) have been known to get to a toll booth in their car and pay for the car behind them as well – sheer grace, and baffling to the recipient! Generosity is infectious, and that's at the heart of the gospel.

For reflection 5

The clothes of the resurrection

It's tricky coming out of a tomb. Particularly if we've settled in and made ourselves quite comfortable.

Many of us are deeply anxious about our identity – who we are and what meaning and value our life really has. So we construct a false self to cover up our nakedness. That false self acts like a series of cloths we wrap around ourselves to try and give ourselves some reality in our own eyes and the eyes of others.

There are many cloths obligingly available. Qualifications are nice and bright; they go with letters after your name and a colourful academic hood. A healthy bank balance – or at least a healthy flow of money through the credit card account – that's a good, substantial cloth to wrap around ourselves as well. Or a full diary, lots of meetings and a general air of importance might convince others that we have a strong identity. We might even convince ourselves some of the time. The accumulation of experiences, of power, of honour, of knowledge – all these things may be useful cloths to wind around ourselves so that we can be sure we really exist.

And then we can be more comfortable in our tombs, because what we've carefully constructed is a false self to cover our nothingness. We've acquired an identity, but it's the identity not of personhood and substance but of colourful cloths. You might call them bandages.

When Jesus stood in front of the grave of Lazarus, he uttered the fearsome command: 'Lazarus, come out!' You can imagine the terrifying pause, and then Lazarus appeared, unwinding the bandages as he came. He couldn't be truly alive and free until he had removed all those restricting cloths.

And nor can we. We have to hear the call of Jesus to come out of our tombs, and to unwrap the defensive strategies we've wound around ourselves. We may not discard our qualifications, bank balance or full diary, but at least we'll stop basing our identity on them. We'll start being honest with ourselves. Then we can stand free in the pure, clear air of the resurrection morning. It feels like a terrible risk to take off these layers of falsity we've built up over the years, but it's the only way to be fully alive as the unique human beings we really are.

And then what are we left with? What have we got on? Perhaps only what Jesus had on (metaphorically) when he emerged from the tomb, which was the all-covering love of God. He had left his grave clothes behind and was identified only by the love of God which had raised him from the dead, not by any acquisitions, honours or qualifications from his previous life in Galilee.

But he was fully alive. And the same can be true of us.

Stations of the resurrection

Many churches are used to the Stations of the Cross, telling the story of Jesus' journey to the cross in fourteen key movements. During Holy Week there are special services following that journey in readings and prayers. What follows here is an adaptation of that basic idea for the resurrection. This is simply an outline with various ideas for how it can be filled out in readings, music, prayers and other material. The outline is intended to be used with the congregation moving to various points of the church for appropriate 'stations'. However, if this is impossible, the service can stand on its own as a kind of 'Resurrection Carol Service', or a representative group can move around the building instead.

A list of possible hymns and songs can be found on pages 109–10. Poems or other readings may be inserted if appropriate, including those in the last section of this book. Everyone will need a printed order of service. Everyone joins in with the words printed in bold.

The service

The service starts in darkness and silence, sustained for a minute. In the darkness a voice prays:

Generous God,
you who raise the dead
and bathe the world in a new and glorious light,
strike our hearts with Easter flame
and set fire to the dry debris of our souls,
that we may blaze with joy
and draw others to your inextinguishable love,
through Jesus Christ our newly risen Lord.

'We are an Easter people'

The lights come on and the first hymn starts immediately.

Hymn *(during which the congregation gather at the altar)*

1 At the altar

Theme: At the tomb

I am the resurrection and the life, says the Lord:
Those who believe in me will never die. Alleluia!

Reading
Luke 24.1–12

Prayer
Eastering God,
who made a holy space in a deadly tomb,
have mercy on our emptiness and fear
and make our empty spaces holy by your risen presence,
through Jesus Christ our Lord. **Amen.**

Praise to you, Lord Jesus:
Dying, you destroyed our death,
rising, you restored our life;
Lord Jesus, come in glory.

2 At the Easter Garden

Theme: The first meeting

Hymn *(during which the congregation move to the Easter garden)*

I am the resurrection and the life, says the Lord:
those who believe in me will never die. Alleluia!

Reading
John 20.1–18

Prayer
Lord Jesus,
you come to our stone-blocked tombs
and offer us life in abundance.
Give us courage to let you roll the stones away
so that light may flood our present darkness.
Then may we rise with you
to our new and dancing day,
for your sake, and for ours. **Amen.**

Praise to you, Lord Jesus:
Dying, you destroyed our death,
rising, you restored our life:
Lord Jesus, come in glory.

3 At a doorway

Theme: The upper room

Hymn *(during which the congregation move to an appropriate closed door)*

I am the resurrection and the life, says the Lord:
those who believe in me will never die. Alleluia!

Reading
John 20.19–29

Prayer
Lord Jesus, risen and let loose in the world,
you come to us even in our darkness and doubt
with words of invitation and welcome.
Continue to reveal yourself to us when doubt is strong and darkness deep,

and in your mercy draw us to safe ground, by the fearless light of faith.
To you be glory and praise for ever. **Amen.**

Praise to you, Lord Jesus:
Dying, you destroyed our death,
rising, you restored our life:
Lord Jesus, come in glory.

4 The central aisle

Theme: The road to Emmaus

Hymn *(during which the congregation move to the front or back of the aisle, with a view of the 'road' ahead)*

I am the resurrection and the life, says the Lord:
those who believe in me will never die. Alleluia!

Reading
Luke 24.13–35

Prayer
Lord Jesus,
we praise and thank you that you are with us
even when we cannot recognize your companionship.
Walk by our side, we pray, as we embark on each day's journey
and walk by the side of the lonely, the burdened and the desperate.
So may our eyes be opened and our hearts burn within us
as you restore hope to our minds and harmony to our hearts.
To you be praise and glory for ever. **Amen.**

Praise to you, Lord Jesus:
Dying, you destroyed our death,
rising, you restored our life:
Lord Jesus, come in glory.

5 At the font

Theme: By the lake

Hymn *(during which the congregation move to the font, the place of water and the discovery and renewal of faith)*

I am the resurrection and the life, says the Lord:
those who believe in me will never die. Alleluia!

Reading
John 20.1–14

Prayer
God of surprises,
you take our breath away by the joy of your rising.
Come to us again with surprise after surprise
so that we learn not to second-guess your actions
but to marvel at their inventiveness,
through him whose surprises give joy to the world,
the one Jesus Christ our Lord. **Amen.**

Praise to you, Lord Jesus:
Dying, you destroyed our death,
rising, you restored our life:
Lord Jesus, come in glory.

6 At the pulpit

Theme: The message of resurrection

Hymn *(during which the congregation gather near the pulpit)*

I am the resurrection and the life, says the Lord:
those who believe in me will never die. Alleluia!

Reading
1 Corinthians 15.1–11

Prayer
Lord Jesus, you are risen from the dead
and we are risen with you.
May our lives reflect the hope and joy
that we find in your resurrection.
Give us strength to defy every kind of oppression
and to oppose every kind of death
in the name of him who silenced death for ever –
you, our Lord and our God. **Amen.**

Praise to you, Lord Jesus:
Dying, you destroyed our death,
rising, you restored our life:
Lord Jesus, come in glory.

7 At the altar

Theme: Christ for the world

Hymn *(during which the congregation return to the altar where they began)*

I am the resurrection and the life, says the Lord:
those who believe in me will never die. Alleluia!

Reading
Matthew 28.16–20

Prayer
Risen Lord Jesus,
you entrusted your mission to followers like us,
frail and uncertain, but trusting in you.
As you commissioned them to go into all the world,
so may all the world come back to you
and give glory to the Father, whose name is praised for ever. **Amen.**

Final hymn

Blessing

The risen Christ go with you on every journey,
strengthen you in every task
and fill you with every lasting joy:
And the blessing of God Almighty, the Father, the Son, and the Holy Spirit, be with you
and those who travel with you, now and always. **Amen.**

A lit candle may be given to everyone in the final hymn to take out as a symbol of the risen Christ moving in and with us into his world.

For reflection 6

The open secret

Resurrection is the secret at the heart of the universe. If we scratch under the surface of any square centimetre of creation new possibilities are lying there, just awaiting their moment. It isn't so much that we have to search endlessly for an occasional gleam of something good, like over-heated gold prospectors panning the river for the discovery that would change their world. The possibilities of renewal are ever-present. God had built resurrection into his world long before he enacted it in the life of Jesus.

That all sounds nice and poetic, but what does it mean?

Well, try this. We see this secret of resurrection in the way our DNA is programmed for healing, rushing reserves to the front as soon as we cut ourselves. We see it in nature's incredible powers of recovery after the drought of a long, hot summer or the devastation of a war. We see it in the caterpillar disappearing into a chrysalis, only to break out later as a butterfly, dazzlingly beautiful and free to fly.

We see resurrection in the couple whose marriage seems to have collapsed irrevocably, but who discover reserves of forgiveness and courage that amaze and delight us. We see it in a community rediscovering self-respect after the devastating closure of its main factory. We see it in a widow making a new life for herself in spite of the tragic experience of loss.

Renewal, redemption, resurrection – they seem to be sewn into the fabric of creation.

In a sense, therefore, what happened on that first resurrection morning wasn't just that Jesus was released from the tomb, but that *we* were released to enter it. We were shown that the empty tomb – the symbol of resurrection – is available for us all to experience. Resurrection is constantly available. It's an open secret. The stone wasn't just rolled away to let Jesus out; it was rolled away to let us in.

One of the eucharistic prayers in the Church of England communion service says it perfectly:

He opened wide his arms for us on the cross;
he put an end to death by dying for us;
and *revealed the resurrection* by rising to new life.

Jesus Christ revealed what was already there – the possibility of a new world.

Why Easter eggs?

It's relatively easy to find symbols for Christmas. You can use a star, a stable, three kings (silhouetted), assorted animals (I once saw a giraffe), and any number of angels singing at the top of their voices. But what have you got to symbolize Easter? A dark cross, dirty nails, a ferocious whip, a vicious crown of thorns, a bloody cloth, a grave – none of it has the same appeal. It just wouldn't go down well in the High Street. So what are we left with?

The answer, it seems, is rabbits and eggs. This is not ideal! Nevertheless, the story of the humble egg does give us some good material for Easter reflection and celebration.

The pre-Christian egg

Pagan use of the egg focused on the many rite-of-spring festivals. The Romans, Chinese, Egyptians and Persians all regarded the egg as a symbol of the universe. As the egg opened up to release new life so it came to represent the rebirth of the earth in the spring. The egg, therefore, was seen to have special creative powers. It was buried under the foundations of buildings to ward off evil; young Roman women carried an egg to help them foretell the sex of their unborn child; brides in Gaul used to step on an egg before crossing the threshold of their new home. Eggs were revered, dyed different colours, and exchanged as special gifts.

The Christian Easter egg

With Christianity the egg came to represent not the rebirth of nature but the rebirth of humanity through the resurrection. The breaking open of the egg reminded Christians of the breaking open of the tomb.

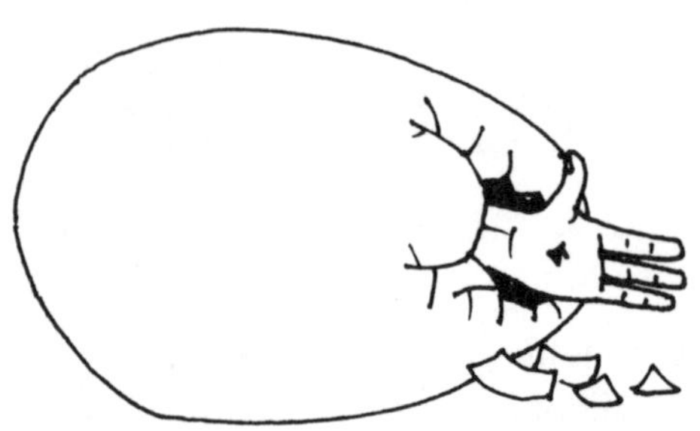

As ever, numerous legends were attached to this powerful symbol. One Polish legend tells of the Virgin Mary giving eggs to the soldiers at the foot of the cross as she begged them to be less cruel to her son. As she wept her tears fell on the eggs, dotting them with brilliant colours. Another Polish legend tells of Mary Magdalene going to the tomb to anoint Jesus' body and taking with her some eggs to keep her going as she undertook her precious task. When she got to the tomb, however, she found that the pure white shells of the eggs had taken on a rainbow of different colours.

Colouring and decorating eggs for Easter came to be part of English custom, too. The household accounts of Edward I for the year 1290 show an expenditure of eighteen pence for 450 eggs to be gold-leafed and coloured for Easter gifts. In some parts of England, families continue to make their Easter picnic an opportunity to enjoy egg rolling competitions, where coloured eggs are rolled down a hill to see whose can go furthest and whose can remain unbroken longest.

The most famous decorated eggs, however, came from Russia. In 1883 the Russian Czar Alexander commissioned Peter Carl Fabergé to make a special Easter gift for his wife, the Empress Marie. The first Fabergé egg was an egg within an egg. The outside shell was platinum, enamelled white, and this opened to reveal a smaller gold egg. This, in turn, opened to display a golden chicken and a jewelled replica of the Imperial Crown. This special egg delighted the Czarina so much that Alexander ordered the Fabergé firm to deliver a new egg each Easter. Fifty-seven eggs were produced in all, and became hugely famous all over the world.

The Easter egg today

In contemporary Greece, eggs are boiled hard, coloured and used in an egg-breaking game. One egg is smashed against another to reveal the winner, and also to symbolize the breaking open of the tomb for each of us.

But it has to be admitted that the chocolate egg now reigns supreme in the West. Commercial pressures and the almost universal enjoyment of chocolate, have led to a massive increase in the range and complexity of chocolate eggs on sale over the Easter period. It seems like the last hold of an ancient symbol on the imagination of the public. But how many children know why they get this annual treat? Perhaps we should tell them.

For reflection 7

Christ is risen (allegedly)

A risen Christ needs a risen Church. If we're serious about the Church being the Body of Christ, then that Church needs to be as risen as its Lord.

So what's gone wrong?

Perhaps we're simply human and can't quite manage to be divine.

Perhaps we believe with our heads but can't quite manage to get it through to our hearts.

Perhaps we've tried to be risen but found it's too tiring.

Perhaps we've tried to be risen, but that was before Mrs Bucket and the argument over the flower stands.

Perhaps we dreamt of the stars but found we were living in the dust.

But maybe we need to be a bit kinder to ourselves in the Church. We constantly analyse our faults and pick at our scabs. We have guilt trips over our guilt trips. We seem to thrive on gloom.

Instead, maybe we could recognize with compassion that we are the *wounded* Body of Christ, wounded by a thousand frailties, but still risen. Maybe, like Peter, we could hear the question afresh from the risen Body of Christ: 'Simon (or Martin or Nicola), do you love me?' And maybe we could say, 'Yes, dear wounded Church, you know that I love you.' And maybe we could mean it and do our best to encourage and strengthen the Church. And maybe this could be wonderful and liberating.

To be a risen Church doesn't mean to be perfect. It means to be a Church sharing the resurrection of the Lord and convinced that this is the way to be fully human and fully alive. We needn't be preoccupied with perfection, but instead we can see the Church as *incorporated* into the risen Christ, part of his risen reality. Our life is 'hidden with Christ in God' (Col. 3.3). When a new son-in-law joins the family, he's incorporated into that family, part of its reality. He doesn't need to be perfect (although it helps, if he's being entrusted with one of my very special daughters!). He's simply valued and loved as part of the family.

The Church, then, isn't just a struggling human institution. Its true identity is as part of the reality of the risen Christ. Its value doesn't depend on our goodness or our ability to be unremittingly holy, and twice as holy on Sundays and Feast Days. It depends on our living in Christ and in his resurrection, and just letting ourselves float in that enormous and mysterious reality.

A risen Christ needs a risen Church, but it will never be a perfect one. We are the wounded Body of Christ – but still risen. So perhaps we could try saying: 'Yes, dear wounded Church, you know that we love you.'

Perhaps we could look at the Church and say – 'Alleluia anyway!'

Just a thought

A MONTH OF DAILY READINGS

The New Testament letters are full of resurrection faith. Sometimes they bubble with it; sometimes they glow with quiet confidence. Here is a series of brief reflections for every day of the month, based on the Easter faith of the New Testament writers. Just take a verse a day (excluding Sundays) and enjoy it!

Day 1

Grace to you and peace from God our Father and the Lord Jesus Christ.
(Phil. 1.2)

This is the way nearly all Paul's letters begin, and you don't send a greeting from someone who's dead. It was the confidence that Christ was alive that enabled Paul to bracket Jesus with the Father as he greeted his friends. Grace is God's active, accepting love; peace was Jesus' parting gift (John 14.27). That's a winning combination for Paul to offer to everyone who was going to read his letters – right down to us. And what we receive we can surely give.

Day 2

To me, living is Christ. *(Phil. 1.21)*

Paul doesn't say 'living is following Christ' or 'imitating Christ' or even 'obeying Christ'. He says living *is* Christ. It's like a new husband saying that living *is* my new wife, so absorbed is he in that relationship. This is the heart of faith – a mystical identity with Christ, an all-embracing union. If we can live through the day with that realization – that our life is totally bound up with the living Lord – then the day is going to be rather special. Even in the difficult moments it will be filled with the presence of Christ.

Day 3

I want to know Christ and the power of his resurrection. (Phil. 3.10)

'Knowing' of this kind is knowing from the inside. It isn't knowing 'about' Christ and the benefits of following him; it's knowing the reality of living in Christ and Christ in us. If that union is the defining form of our faith then the possibilities of resurrection simply start to flow through us. Life may not be easy, but it will never be without hope because the resurrection is a rock-bottom guarantee against despair. Put the template of resurrection over any dilemma and the hard surface begins to melt. The presence of the risen Christ is more powerful than we can imagine.

Day 4

So if you have been raised with Christ, seek the things that are above, where Christ is, seated at the right hand of God. (Col. 3.1)

Seeking the things that are above doesn't mean being so heavenly minded that we're no earthly use. It means living with the largest backdrop possible, an eternal one, rather than living with our eyes fixed on the pavement and the shop windows. It also means setting our sights on what Paul describes in Philippians as 'whatever is true, honourable, just and pure' – the hallmarks of the coming kingdom of God. It's not a call to be pious; it's a call to be holy, and true holiness is about dealing with the dirt and the dust of life as well as the gold and the glory.

Day 5

When you were buried with him in baptism, you were also raised with him through faith in the power of God, who raised him from the dead. (Col. 2.12)

In Paul's time baptism meant a full descent into the water, symbolizing death by drowning. The old selfish personality had been finished off, and the new self could erupt from the water, escaping the chaos and gulping in new life. It was a dramatic picture of what being 'raised with Christ' really meant. That's all rather a long way from our conventional, domestic view of baptism as a rite of passage ('Have you remembered the camera?' 'She was as good as gold until the vicar poured all that water over her'). Perhaps we should reconsider baptism as a life-changing event. When faced with difficulties Luther was fond of saying, definitively: 'I have been baptized!'

Day 6

Your life is hidden with Christ in God. *(Col. 3.2)*

To be hidden doesn't necessarily mean to be running away. A soldier is hidden in camouflaged battledress in order to be secure, not to avoid the action. Similarly, to be hidden with Christ in God means to be in the safest possible place to do dangerous things. Christians have always been found in the toughest places doing the hardest tasks because they live with the risen Christ in the heart of God, and can therefore afford to take risks. And even those of us who live quieter lives can take risks of faith almost every day. But will we?

Day 7

God put this power to work in Christ when he raised him from the dead and seated him at his right hand in the heavenly places. *(Eph. 1.20)*

When God 'put this power to work in Christ, [raising] him from the dead', it was as if the engine of creation was suddenly thrown into reverse. This power is huge, and it's the power that could set Jesus in the heavenly places. But it's also the power that Christians can just begin to touch today. It's not that we can do magic but we can 'go with the grain' of God, the Lord of resurrection, and so discover our God-given potential. What would it be like today if 'God put this power to work' in us?

Day 8

Even when we were dead through our trespasses, [God] made us alive together with Christ. (Eph. 2.5)

Paul is making a point about humanity collectively, but it also applies personally. Most people carry around a considerable amount of buried guilt, like discarded iron in the soul. But God swaps that heavy weight for the gift of life, inviting us to share the freedom of Jesus Christ. The heart of the heart of the gospel is the forgiveness of sins. As someone who had experienced it wrote to me: 'Forgiveness displaces our darkness, changes how we are inside, changes how we feel, calms us down, changes the things around us, has power to change the world.' As Paul would have said, 'God makes us alive together with Christ.'

Day 9

Now in Christ Jesus you who once were far off have been brought near by the blood of Christ. For he is our peace. (Eph. 2.13–14)

There's a lot of restlessness in our society. Perhaps the next job, the next relationship, the next experience will give us satisfaction and peace. Or perhaps not. We carry around our own distress. We need to be part of something bigger that can embrace and dissolve our anxiety and restlessness. Here's the answer: Christ is our peace. He's absorbed our sorrows in his death and brought us home to the *shalom* of God. He's taken humanity beyond the distress of life and death. He's taken hold of the future so that we can relax in the present. Christ is our peace.

Day 10

'Sleeper, awake! Rise from the dead, and Christ will shine on you.' (Eph. 5.14)

There's a difference between crawling out of bed reluctantly to face a day's work, and leaping out of bed on holiday for a day in the sun. Christians are fortunate enough to know that any and every day the love of Christ will be shining fully on them. And yet there's still a choice – we still have to get out of bed! We still have to be attentive to

God and ready for action. Christians who remain asleep when there's so much to enjoy are wasting their birthright.

Day 11

Who was . . . declared to be Son of God with power according to the spirit of holiness by resurrection from the dead, Jesus Christ our Lord.

(Rom. 1.3–4)

If you were in any doubt about who Jesus is, here's the proof that he really is the Son of God: he was raised from the dead. Resurrection is a pretty conclusive argument. We may have questions; we may ask how it happened; but if someone is raised from the dead at least we have to take notice. Not that we'll ever fully understand it – that's not the point. But let's stop worrying about incidentals. The big question is this: did Jesus rise from the dead? Because if he did, our lives can't stay the same. Alleluia!

Day 12

We know that Christ, being raised from the dead, will never die again: death no longer has dominion over him. *(Rom. 6.9)*

'You only live twice.' Jesus was raised to life from what seemed like a disastrous death, and since it's God who's done this, there's no question of him dying again. This second life after death is for ever. And since Christians live 'in Christ', covered by the life of Christ, that second life will be ours too. What's more, we anticipate that life in the present – Christians live in Easter Day, not Good Friday.

Day 13

If the Spirit of him who raised Jesus from the dead dwells in you, he who raised Christ from the dead will give life to your mortal bodies also through his Spirit that dwells in you. *(Rom. 8.11)*

In this one verse Paul writes of divine activity as being *from* God, *in* Jesus and coming *through* the Spirit. The Christian understanding of the Trinity is already beginning to take shape. And whereas elsewhere Paul writes of Christ being in us (and we in him), here he writes of the *Spirit* dwelling in us. This is the reality of daily Christian living – God's Spirit being in us and giving us 'life' in the richest Christian sense. Remembering that one central fact – that the Spirit of Jesus is living in us – might be the most transforming conviction we have. Not just words but reality. Not just a concept but the very energy of God.

Day 14

Who will separate us from the love of Christ? *(Rom. 8.35)*

The final verses of this chapter ring out with Christian conviction. Nothing in life or death, in hell or high water, can separate the Christian believer from the risen Lord. This is the confidence with which people have gone into battle with bullets whistling past their head, or into the operating theatre with the odds stacked the wrong way. What's promised them isn't a VC or perfect health. What's promised is simply Christ and his inexhaustible love. If that has proved sufficient for so many, might it not also be the same for us? The love of Christ will see us through today and any other day we choose to share with him.

Day 15

You are not lacking in any spiritual gift as you wait for the revealing of our Lord Jesus Christ. *(1 Cor. 1.7)*

The lights go down; the audience hushes; the anticipation is intense; we wait for the curtain to go up, for the stage to be revealed and the action to start. So we wait for the risen Christ to be finally revealed in his glory – truly, marvellously, the Lord of heaven and earth. Quite how this will actually happen defies any human attempt at description, but it will be worth waiting for. In the meantime there's a job to be done preparing the stage and setting up the lighting. Nothing we do can bring it on, but everything we do can be done in preparation.

Day 16

I handed on to you as of first importance what I in turn had received: that Christ died for our sins in accordance with the scriptures, and that he was buried, and that he was raised on the third day in accordance with the scriptures. (1 Cor. 15.3–4)

The death and resurrection of Jesus are 'of first importance'. Christians mustn't shy away from these events and confine themselves to commending the life and teaching of Jesus. We have to keep the main things the main things. And Paul is anxious to point out (he does it twice) that these happened as the scriptures had said they would. They had been pointing in this direction all along and now they'd exploded into life. Has our faith exploded into life too, through the death and resurrection of Jesus? Because that's also 'of first importance'.

Day 17

Last of all, as to one untimely born, he appeared also to me. (1 Cor. 15.8)

Paul has listed the appearances of Jesus to his disciples and others in the days and weeks after Easter. Then, greatly daring, he puts into the list his own experience of meeting the risen Christ on the road to his new life. We, greatly daring, might do the same. The risen Christ 'appears' to us in ways that are utterly unique, but those experiences are never to be disallowed. Someone with an experience is never at the mercy of someone with an argument. But we have to own and value the experience of Christ that we, personally, have been given.

Day 18

If for this life only we have hoped in Christ, we are of all people most to be pitied. (1 Cor. 15.19)

The resurrection of Jesus is good news for both this life and the next. There's no limit to the goodness of the good news. It hasn't just given us a little more hope in the gathering gloom; it's assured us of a whole new world breaking in from the future. And our response to that shouldn't just be a few minor rearrangements in our domestic routines; this calls for a root and branch reassessment of who we are and what we do and where we're going. And that's a task made up of daily details. There are indeed two lives – this one and the next – but we have to take them one at a time.

Day 19

Thanks be to God, who gives us the victory through our Lord Jesus Christ.
(1 Cor. 15.57)

Paul has been working his way through a complex argument in this chapter. At the end he simply bursts out with the burning core of his faith – Christ has given us the victory! History seemed to be running away from God, but now the process is reversed, evil is on the run and the forces of death have left the field in disorder. The invitation of Jesus is clear: 'Why not join the winning side?' But the great victory has to be translated into a hundred smaller ones as we engage with our own temptations and trivialities – today.

Day 20

The Son of God, Jesus Christ, whom we proclaimed among you . . . was not 'Yes and No': but in him it is always 'Yes'. For in him every one of God's promises is a 'Yes'. *(2 Cor. 1.19–20)*

Paul is so bowled over by the fact and reality of the resurrection that it's forever slipping into his writing and thinking. In these verses it slips out as the conviction that God is always saying 'yes' to his people; it's what he promised and so it's what he does. And this is part of God's great 'yes' to his creation, as he tries to encourage everything and everyone into fulfilling more of their God-given potential. The same is true of us. He says 'yes' to us and our uniqueness, urging us to succeed. And we say . . . ?

Day 21

If anyone is in Christ there is a new creation: everything old has passed away; see, everything has become new! (2 Cor. 5.17)

Christians have a new passport. It says that we belong to a new kingdom and are ambassadors for a new king. It's hard to live with that reality, but it's harder still to live without it. In the midst of this world's multiple sorrows it's important to have a resurrection perspective so we don't get submerged. Moreover, Paul tells Christians that they're a crucial part of God's new creation and, by their conversion and their actions, are supposed to anticipate the transformation of all things at the end of time. Being transformed isn't a job for an hour on a Sunday morning; that kind of makeover takes a lifetime and it needs a Saviour.

Day 22

Now may the God of peace, who brought back from the dead our Lord Jesus, the great shepherd of the sheep, by the blood of the eternal covenant, make you complete in everything good so that you may do his will.

(Heb. 13.20–1)

The resurrection provides the filter through which the first Christians saw everything. So when the writer to the Hebrews is wishing his hearers well, he naturally includes another reference to Jesus being raised from the dead. The writer's main point is that this God whose power is sufficient to raise Christ from the dead can also work wonders in our lives – he can 'complete' the possibilities for good that lie in our own personalities. It's a ravishing vision – all of us 'perfect in every good work'. But visions can become realities when God is truly allowed to get to work in us.

Day 23

Blessed be the God and Father of our Lord Jesus Christ! By his great mercy he has given us a new birth into a living hope through the resurrection of Jesus Christ from the dead, and into an inheritance that is imperishable, undefiled and unfading. (1 Pet. 1.3–4)

These verses reverberate with passionate confidence. Image is followed by image: a new birth, a living hope, a rock-solid legacy. This was the confidence that enabled the first Christians to face terrible persecution when it came. Our faith tends to be so much more measured and qualified; you wonder whether there's anything we would truly die for. And then we find that more Christians than ever today are paying the ultimate price for their faith, sometimes in the places to which we go on holiday. Lord, have mercy.

Day 24

The one who testifies to these things says, 'Surely I am coming soon.' Amen. Come, Lord Jesus! *(Rev. 22.20)*

The one who comes is indeed coming at the end of history, but he has already come in the midst of history, and he comes every day to encounter his people. The one who comes is the creator of joy and justice and he's looking for partners. The one who comes is alive, returned from the dead, never to be shackled again. The one who comes isn't put off by our lack of welcome, but nevertheless he looks for our Amen, our 'yes'. The one who comes has loved us from the beginning of time. Even so, come, Lord Jesus.

For reflection 8

Hungry for life

What exploded out of the tomb that Easter morning was life. Until then the story was about death. Suddenly the narrative has lurched radically in another direction. Reality has shifted on its axis. Life has burst out of a tomb.

Sadly, the word hasn't got around. Not everywhere, anyway. The word is 'life'. Not 'religion', not 'church', not even 'Christianity'. What Jesus promised, and what he delivered, was 'life'. And this life isn't just a religious consumable for a specialist market. It's a gift for the world. 'In him was life,' says the prologue to St John's Gospel, 'and that life was the light of all people.' Note the 'all people'. This is the life, the energy, that fuels the world, not just the Church.

Just a few weeks earlier, among other things, Jesus had been promising life in all its fullness. Now here it is – freshly minted in the fires of resurrection. The words of John V. Taylor ring profoundly true: 'It has long been my conviction that God is not hugely concerned as to whether we are religious or not. What matters to God, and matters supremely, is whether we are alive or not.' Consequently we have to look at our faith and very honestly decide whether it's bringing us more fully to life, or whether, in subtle ways, it's actually diminishing us. If it's the latter, we can be sure that God will not be in it. Nor will Jesus.

Unfortunately some expressions of faith seem to be designed with uncanny accuracy to nail 'life' down and keep God firmly in his place. Perhaps it feels too dangerous to release the lion that roars in the night, the magnificent marauding God from whom no-one is safe, but with whom everyone is secure.

Of course, life like this should not be confused with cheap-and-cheerful pleasure-seeking. The life that erupts from a tomb is an altogether more serious, full-bodied vintage. This kind of life doesn't come cheap; it comes with the full cost of a cross, with the result that it attempts to find a way of handling dark-ness, tragedy and death. No easy escape route here; no fast track to fantasy.

The resurrection, ultimately, is for people who are hungry for life. It's for those who are prepared to come alive to the vast, embracing love of God, to the glory and tragedy of the world, to the potential of Christ within each of us.

But without the resurrection, we would never have known . . .

Reflections

JOHN 20 AND 21 FOR TODAY

This is a meditative journey through the resurrection narratives in John 20 and 21. It can be used for personal reflection or adapted for group use. The method employed is that of reflective questions, set alongside some of the key incidents in the narrative. The aim here is not to offer a detailed Bible study but rather to let the story prompt personal reflection and insight.

> 20.1 *Early on the first day of the week, while it was still dark . . .*

John presents the resurrection as a journey from darkness to sight. (See also the blind man in John 9 coming to believe – to 'see' – increasingly clearly, just as the Pharisees become more and more blind.) Mary and the disciples see and believe more and more clearly as the light dawns in their hearts. The resurrection isn't a mighty act in John but a quiet rising of the sun which has already defeated the darkness (on the cross). Is that our experience of faith? How did we first come to 'see' the importance or the truth of faith?

> 20.6 *Then Simon Peter came, following him, and went into the tomb. He saw the linen wrappings lying there, and the cloth that had been on Jesus' head, not lying with the linen wrappings but rolled up in a place by itself. Then the other disciple, who reached the tomb first, also went in, and he saw and believed.*

This is a very vivid description. It suggests that the linen wrappings had collapsed in on themselves, not been removed and thrown aside. There's even the detail that the cloth which would have been over Jesus' head was separate from the rest, leaving a gap where the neck would have been. How important is this kind of detail for us? Do we find ourselves trying to work out what happened and how it could have happened, or do we leave that to others?

20.11 But Mary stood weeping outside the tomb.

The Greek word for 'stood' means 'rooted'. She was grief-stricken and paralysed. By the end of the story she's 'uprooted' and on the move, rushing back to find the disciples (v. 18). As Mary realizes what's happened, she's transformed. Does our faith set us free and mobilize us like that? What has our faith led us into doing for others? Does it sometimes have the opposite effect, constricting and diminishing us, and if so, what can we do to reclaim our freedom?

20.13 'They have taken away my Lord . . .'

In verse 2, when Mary went to tell Peter and the 'other disciple', she said they had taken away 'the' Lord. Now they have taken away 'my' Lord. Jesus was terribly important to her and she's increasingly desperate as she realizes what she's lost. How personal is our relationship with Jesus Christ? What could we do to deepen it?

20.15 Jesus said to her, 'Woman, why are you weeping? Whom are you looking for?'

Jesus' first words after the resurrection are a question – almost the same question as his first words in the Gospel, spoken to John's disciples, 'What are you looking for?' (John 1.38). Jesus takes our needs and our perception of them with the utmost seriousness. What are we really looking for in faith and in life? Do we articulate those needs to Jesus?

20.16 Jesus said to her 'Mary!' She turned and said to him in Hebrew 'Rabbouni!' (which means Teacher). Jesus said to her, 'Do not hold on to me, because I have not yet ascended to the Father.'

Jesus' words must have been hard for Mary. She longed for the reassuring touch, the familiar presence of Jesus, the man she loved. But Jesus can't let her hold on to the past. His is a new order, a new world, and physical presence cannot be the criterion for intimacy in such a new reality. Do we not find, as well, that physical presence can sometimes hinder true knowing? Sometimes too much detail gets in the way of deeper understanding. True appreciation of someone can often develop better with a little distance, and absence can lead to a deeper presence. The truth is that love lets go. Love releases. Mary needed to let Jesus go so that he would no longer be simply 'with' her but could be a part of her, 'in' her, working through her, by his Spirit. Are we prepared to believe that we may become closer to some people through their absence? Has that happened to us? Has the 'absence' of Jesus sometimes been painful?

> *20.19 When it was evening on that day, the first day of the week, and the doors of the house where the disciples had met were locked for fear of the Jews . . .*

The doors were understandably locked. What had happened to Jesus might well happen to the disciples too. But through this, Jesus might have been locked out as well. We lock our doors mainly because of fear – fear of failure, of being rumbled, of being unacceptable, of clumsiness, ignorance, sin – but in so doing we may be locking out Jesus too, the One we need. What makes us lock Jesus out? What are the no-go areas in our lives? What can we do about it?

> *20.19 Jesus came and stood among them and said 'Peace be with you.'*

Although the disciples tried to lock everyone and everything out, Jesus still appeared in their midst. He came through the man-made barrier they had created. His task was too important to be held back. His greeting was simple but profound: 'Peace be with you.' He said it twice. Jesus knew that fear is the biggest barrier to our flourishing. Even the most confident people usually admit to major fears that sometimes almost cripple them. In saying 'Peace be with you,' Jesus was saying the disciples had nothing to fear. The One who said this had been to the far extremities of human experience – and come back. So he had the authority to say, 'I've been there and I'm with you, so there's nothing to fear.' Can we trust that promise in the area of our greatest fears? How would we try to claim that promise and live it out?

> *20.21 Jesus said to them again, 'Peace be with you.'*

With the peace of Christ they have nothing to fear. The phrase 'Do not be afraid' occurs more times on the lips of Jesus than any other, and in the whole Bible it is said to occur 365 times (what does that suggest!).

To be filled with this peace is to be filled with Jesus. Can we imagine being filled with the Spirit of Jesus, whose love will cast out our fears?

> *20.21–2 'As the Father has sent me, so I send you.' When he had said this, he breathed on them and said to them, 'Receive the Holy Spirit.'*

In Genesis 2.7 we have the same image – God breathed into the first man the breath of life. Now Jesus breathes into the disciples the new life of the Spirit – his Spirit. This is nothing less than a new creation. 'If anyone is in Christ there is a new creation' (2 Cor. 5.17) – if anyone is in Christ, and if Christ is in them. We may not feel like a new creation on a Monday morning in January, but could we try to breathe in this new life even then? And at the start of every day?

> *20.24 Thomas (who was called the Twin), one of the twelve, was not with them when Jesus came. So the other disciples told him, 'We have seen the Lord.'*

We aren't told who Thomas' twin was, so that allows us to claim the privilege! Thomas is our twin, and the twin of all who have doubts and want to be sure. Do we dare risk owning our doubts, even to ourselves? What do we struggle with? Is that OK? (Remember Thomas was still 'one of the twelve'.)

> *20.25 He said to them, 'Unless I see the mark of the nails in his hands, and put my finger in the mark of the nails and my hand in his side, I will not believe.'*

Thomas had too much riding on the truth of this fantastic tale. He was actually a passionate disciple, urging his friends to go and die with Jesus if necessary (John 11.16). So he had to be sure. Thomas stands between the disciples and ourselves; he is part of both, and part of us all. Again we see the link in John between seeing and believing – as at the start of the chapter and in chapter 9 – to believe is to 'see' clearly and fully. Jesus' final words in this incident are crucial: 'Blessed are those who have not seen and yet have come to believe.' That's us! How much 'proof' do we need, and how much are we prepared to 'see with the heart'?

21.1–3 After these things Jesus showed himself again to the disciples by the Sea of Tiberias . . . Simon Peter said . . . 'I am going fishing.'

Seven of the disciples returned to Galilee and decided to go fishing again. They turned to the familiar old world when their new world crashed around them. What else were they to do? Something had changed but they weren't sure what. Jesus seemed to be around the place but they couldn't get hold of what it was all about. Have we ever had the experience of not knowing quite what's going on and feeling bewildered by it all? When it all gets too much for us, what familiar places and activities do we return to?

21.4 Just after daybreak, Jesus stood on the beach; but the disciples did not know that it was Jesus.

Jesus doesn't impose his presence. Again it's that mysterious early dawn – John signalling that again the disciples are going to travel from darkness to sight, from confusion to belief. Having our eyes open isn't enough; we need an openness of spirit to recognize the thrilling presence of the risen Lord. Would it be true that our spiritual eyes are often half closed and unexpectant? What does it mean to recognize the risen Christ?

21.6–7 He said to them, 'Cast the net to the right side of the boat and you will find some.' So they cast it, and now they were not able to haul it in because there were so many fish. That disciple whom Jesus loved said to Peter, 'It is the Lord!' When Simon Peter heard that it was the Lord, he put on some clothes, for he was naked, and jumped into the sea.

The right side of the boat is the side of blessing. So obedience brings its reward. It's the eyes of love that recognize Jesus – those of the beloved disciple. But it's impetuous Peter who wants to leap into the sea to get to the Lord. Love like Peter's is prepared to get out of the boat, to do the unconventional thing, to take a risk. This was the start of Peter's rehabilitation after his shocking denial on that terrible night in Jerusalem. Have we ever 'got out of the boat' for love of Christ? What happened? Have we ever sunk in taking such a risk, and what did Jesus do then?

21.10 Jesus said to them, 'Bring some of the fish that you have just caught.' So Simon Peter went aboard and hauled the net ashore, full of large fish, a hundred and fifty-three of them; and though there were so many, the net was not torn.

John's readers will have taken the huge catch to be the future growth of the fledgling Church. The number 153 might be the numbers 1 to 17 all added up, with 17 being made up of the perfect number 7 and the number 10 representing fullness. The net was not torn because it isn't the will of Jesus that there be any divisions in his Church. Are we part of any dissension in the Church? Why might we, or others, get so angry when things don't go our way in church? How can we contribute to healing divisions in our own church?

21.12–13 Jesus said to them, 'Come and have breakfast.' . . . Jesus came and took the bread and gave it to them, and did the same with the fish.

The eating together was a reminder of the Last Supper where Jesus took the bread, gave thanks, broke it and shared it. Communion was restored among the little group of Jesus' friends. No words were used for this act of reconciliation; Jesus wasn't into recrimination. He simply wanted to restore the fellowship of the disciples. Have we experienced the sacramental power of eating together? Have we known the joy of being taken back into a friendship?

21.15 When they had finished breakfast, Jesus said to Simon Peter, 'Simon son of John, do you love me more than these?' He said to him, 'Yes, Lord; you know that I love you.'

The scene takes place by a charcoal fire, just as Peter's denial took place by another charcoal fire. Jesus heals Peter's paralysed memory, not by interrogation and making Peter grovel, but by using a liberating question about love. He knows what's best in Peter and he goes back to that passionate heart. 'Do you love me?' No blame; nor does he ask for any guarantees from Peter. Jesus doesn't operate in a framework of law but rather of grace. Have we ever known the liberating effect of returning to Christ with a full heart? Have we realized, in the roots of our being, that our relationship with God is based on love and grace, and not on 'doing the right things'?

21.15 Jesus said to him, 'Feed my lambs.'

Jesus immediately gave Peter a major responsibility. There was no probationary period: he simply gave Peter the main task of caring for the little Church that was being born. Peter knew that to be given this responsibility didn't mean he was to play a role; he was not any better than anyone else. He was not even being asked whether he was strong or an inspiring preacher or had good organizational skills. He was simply asked whether he loved Jesus, and then he was given the major task of caring for the faithful community. Do we accept our responsibilities in the Church and in life generally as an expression of love, a way of serving people because we love Jesus Christ? Have we seen these tasks as given to us by the risen Lord?

21.19 After this he said to him, 'Follow me.'

Will we?

Part Three

MAKING THE MOST OF THE RESURRECTION

Courses, prayers and poetry

Small group courses 1

THE RESURRECTION IN THE GOSPELS

Many churches are used to Lent courses. They may even run to Advent courses. But one good way of letting the Easter message enter our bloodstream is to have a course running in the two months after Easter.

What follows, in this and the next section, are two series of courses, each of four sessions, which might be adopted or adapted for use in home groups, cells or youth groups. They might also be adapted for a dayaway, a quiet day or a church weekend.

Of course, the series could be used at any other time of year as well. The resurrection is always happening 'now'!

Home group course

The resurrection according to Matthew

1 Light a candle in the middle of the group.
The leader says: 'Alleluia. Christ is risen!'
All reply: **'He is risen indeed. Alleluia!'**

2 Explain that the session runs through a Starter, the Story, various Spin-offs and then Space for prayer.

3 **Starter:**
Share experiences, stories, conversations from the past week which had about them a sense of resurrection, a feel of new life. These could be events in family life, events in the lives of others (including those in the public eye this week), developments in church life, a glimpse of hope in the natural world or in a person's attitude to a problem – indeed, anything which speaks of resurrection. Let this run for a reasonable time, because sharing experience and making

Mislaying his hot cross bun had spoilt Hugh's whole Easter

links between faith and everyday life can be one of the most rewarding parts of the group's life. This exercise should take place at the start of each of the four Gospel sessions, thereby building up the members' confidence in recognizing 'resurrection events' in everyday life.

4 **Story**: read Matthew 28.
Questions:
(a) Split the group into three sub-groups: the priests and elders, the guards, the disciples. Ask them to consider in their group for

10–15 minutes what they would want to say to the other two groups or what questions they would want to ask them. Then lead a guided conversation between the groups, enabling each to question and challenge the others.

(b) Other groups might have been accused of stealing the body, e.g. the Roman authorities or the Jewish authorities. What arguments could be assembled for and against those views? The arguments could be charted up.

(c) In Matthew's account, when the women met the risen Christ they held on to his feet (v. 9). In John's account, Mary Magdalene is specifically told by Jesus not to hold on to him (John 20.17). What truths are contained in both these stories?

(d) Ask people how their understanding of what happened that Easter morning has changed in the light of the discussion so far.

5 **Spin-offs:**

(a) Who demonstrated to you by word or action that Christ is risen? How do you try to demonstrate that to others, or how might you do so?

(b) Jesus said, 'Go and make disciples.' Jot down individually three things your church could do to obey that commission better than it does. Share the ideas in the group, but then get practical. Who would do each task, and should some other activities be stopped or put on hold? Who will you pass these ideas on to?

6 **Space for prayer:**

(a) Have a dark bag with some stones in it. Observe that most of us have things which remain in the dark – things we are sorry for, things we struggle with, hurts which never get out into daylight. These things remain in the darkness of the tomb. Then hand round the bag and invite people to take out one stone each and let it be for them something they would like to bring out into the light or from which they would like to be released. Give space and silence for reflection. Pray a prayer of thanksgiving that the risen Christ enables us to bring the dark secrets out of our tombs (even if, as yet, we may not be able to speak about them to others). Invite people to take the stone home and maybe leave it in the garden – in the light.

(b) Scatter around the lighted candle some small cards on which are various gifts that flow out of the resurrection, e.g.:
   (i) '**Peace** be with you' (John 20.19).
   (ii) '**Do not be afraid**' (Matt. 28.5).
   (iii) 'Receive the **Holy Spirit**' (John 20.22).
   (iv) 'Remember, **I am with you** always' (Matt. 28.20).
   (v) 'They . . . returned to Jerusalem with great **joy**' (Luke 24.52).
   (vi) **Confidence** in Christ. 'So they cast [the net], and now they were not able to haul it in' (John 21.6).
   (vii) **Blessing.** 'Blessed are those who have not seen and yet have come to believe' (John 20.29).
   (viii) **Hope.** 'He has given us a new birth into a living hope through the resurrection of Jesus Christ from the dead' (1 Pet. 1.3).

There could be many more. Cards can of course be duplicated so there are enough for everyone.

Ask each member of the group to take a card, and then, when each has one, ask them to give thanks or to pray about that gift of the resurrection – in relation to the group, individuals in need, or the world. If they simply want to read the verse on the card and be silent, then of course that's fine too. Then offer a gathering-up prayer in gratitude for all the gifts that flow from the resurrection of Jesus from the dead. This form of prayer can be repeated at each session.

7 **Ending:**
Leader: Go in the light and peace of Christ. Alleluia, alleluia!
All: **Thanks be to God. Alleluia, alleluia!**
Then blow out the candle.

Home group course

The resurrection according to Mark

1 Light a candle in the middle of the group.
Leader: 'Alleluia. Christ is risen!'
All: **'He is risen indeed. Alleluia!'**

2 Explain again that the session runs through a Starter, the Story, various Spin-offs and then Space for prayer.

3 **Starter:**
As in the Matthew session, share experiences, stories, conversations, events from the last week which had echoes of resurrection about them. Encourage members of the group to link the gospel reality of resurrection to the reality of daily experience.

4 **Story**: read Mark 16.1–20.
Questions:
(a) Look at the ending of Mark 16 (verses 9–20) and evaluate it. Does it ring true? If not, why not? What might have happened?
(b) 'They had been saying to one another, "Who will roll away the stone?"' Can you imagine what else they may have been saying to one another?
(c) 'They saw a young man, dressed in a white robe.' As a twenty-first-century Christian, how do you evaluate these angelic appearances?
(d) The young man told them to tell the disciples that Jesus was going ahead of them to Galilee but 'they said nothing to anyone'. Why did they disobey?

5 **Spin-offs:**
(a) We read in verse 8 that the women fled from the tomb, terrified and amazed, and 'they said nothing to anyone, for they were afraid'. On what occasions have you been terrified? What happened? Did your faith help? (Be honest!)
(b) How many different types of fear can we identify? What is the difference between them, and how can each be faced? How effective is the word of the angel: 'Do not be alarmed'?

(c) Have we ever lost the ending of something important, or been cut off in our prime? What did we do? How can the 'lost ending' of something be redeemed?
(d) 'He is going ahead of you to Galilee.' What are the 'Galilees' we want Jesus to go into ahead of us at present?

6 **Space for prayer:**
(a) Give each member of the group a piece of paper – dark-coloured if possible. Remind them of the words of the angel: 'Do not be afraid.' Ask them to write on their paper anything of which they are afraid (even if it's hard to see because of the colour of the paper). Assure them no-one will see what they have written. If there's no smoke alarm in the place and it's quite safe, ask people to come forward in their own time and burn the piece of paper in the candle flame, letting the fear be taken away in the light of Christ's risen presence. If there's any doubt about fire safety, have the group come forward and tear their pieces of paper into small pieces and leave them scattered at the base of the candle with the assurance that they will be thrown away or burnt straight after the session. End with a prayer invoking the promise of Christ that we need not be afraid. The most common thing said by Jesus and the angel(s) after the resurrection was 'Do not be afraid.'
(b) As in the Matthew session, scatter around the lighted candle some small cards on which are written various gifts that flow out of the resurrection (see p. 94). The members of the group pray with, and out of, the card they have picked up, or they read the promised gift and leave space for silent prayer. The leader gathers the prayers together at the end.
(c) Invite members of the group to pray for each other and the 'Galilees' others have mentioned in the previous discussion – those places where we want Jesus to have gone before us.

7 **Ending:**
Leader: Go in the peace of Christ. Alleluia, alleluia!
All: **Thanks be to God. Alleluia, alleluia!**
Then blow out the candle.

Small group course

The resurrection according to Luke

This session is based on the walk to Emmaus and can be adapted to take up a whole quiet day, church dayaway or part of a weekend, as well as a single evening.

1 Light a candle in the middle of the group.
Leader: Alleluia. Christ is risen!
All: **He is risen indeed. Alleluia!**

2 Explain that the session runs through the normal sequence of a Starter, the Story, various Spin-offs and Space for prayer, but on this occasion the content of each element is somewhat different from that of the sessions on Matthew and Mark. But nothing to worry about!

3 **Starter**: an Emmaus walk.
The sharing of experience this time isn't about echoes of the resurrection during the last week or two but, like the two disciples on the road to Emmaus, a sharing in pairs of experiences of disappointment. What did those disappointments feel like? How did you cope with them at the time? What did you learn from them? The disciples had been reflecting sadly on their high hopes for the impact of Jesus on their nation's life ('We had hoped that he would be the one to redeem Israel'). Have you ever felt similarly let down – personally, in a group, in a church, or nationally? And how did you pull out of this experience? How was Jesus present? What did you come to understand better as a result of it all?

Ideally this exercise is done in pairs out walking together through a large garden, a park, or in the grounds of a retreat centre. If this isn't possible, privacy has to be guaranteed in order to encourage trust and honesty.

4 **Story**: read Luke 24.13–35.
Questions:
(a) What might it mean that the disciples were 'kept from recognizing' Jesus (v. 16)?

(b) He 'was a prophet mighty in deed and word before God and all the people' (v. 19). How might different groups of people have been seeing Jesus at this particular time? For example, what would the disciples have said about him, about who he was and what he was doing? And what would the Jewish authorities have said, and the people, and the Romans? Would all the disciples have said the same thing? What might we have been saying if we'd been there?

(c) In spite of the women saying that the tomb was empty and Jesus was alive (vv. 22–4), the disciples had set off for Emmaus in despair. Why?

(d) Jesus interpreted the scriptures to the disciples (v. 27), pointing out the references to himself. What would we point to in particular? And how much credibility do we place in apparently prophetic verses in the Old Testament?

(e) 'He took bread, blessed and broke it, and gave it to them. Then their eyes were opened' (v. 30). What does it really mean for us to recognize Jesus in the breaking of the bread?

5 **Spin-offs**: the Emmaus meal.

Now is the time to eat together. This could take the form of a straightforward meal, an agape or a communion service, whichever is appropriate. A *meal* would give the opportunity for simple friendship and the sharing of gifts. An *agape* would take the form of the sharing of bread and wine at a central point in the meal as symbols of fellowship, but without the words of consecration which set those elements apart in a full eucharistic context. A *communion* would be pared down to the essentials but would draw out the full implications of what Jesus did at that Emmaus supper table.

6 **Space for prayer:**

(a) In some groups it might be possible to return to the pairs at the start and, with that person, to pray about what has been learned and experienced.

(b) There has been much talking. There could now be an extended silence of anything from five minutes upwards, while people are invited to reflect, pray, rest or respond to the stimulus of the session.

(c) As we return to our 'Jerusalems' we could take our own determinations and intentions. 'How do we want to respond to all of this? What do we want to do or to promise?' These intentions could be written down on cards and held towards the lighted candle (the symbol of Christ's risen presence) while a prayer of corporate offering is made by the leader.

7 **Ending:**
Leader: Go in the light and peace of Christ. Alleluia, alleluia!
All: **Thanks be to God. Alleluia, alleluia!**
Then blow out the candle.

Small group course

The resurrection according to John

John's account of the resurrection contains much rich material. If only one evening session is available, it may prove necessary to focus on one or two of the scenes John offers. On the other hand there may be material here for a dayaway, a quiet day or a church weekend.

1 Light a candle in the middle of the group.
Leader: Alleluia. Christ is risen!
All: **He is risen indeed. Alleluia!**

2 Explain that the session runs through the normal sequence of a Starter, the Story, various Spin-offs and Space for prayer, but that (maybe) you're having to focus on particular parts of the Gospel account.

3 **Starter:**
   (a) *Either*: share experiences, stories, conversations, events from the last week which had about them echoes of resurrection and new life.
   (b) *Or*: each member of the group is asked to describe a favourite place next to water – a lakeside, a sea shore, a river bank. Such places are often associated with significant events or experiences, and the places people choose to share will turn out to be fascinating – I almost guarantee it!

4 **Story:** read John 20 and 21, or parts, as appropriate.
Three scenes are available for study and discussion. Any one, two or all three can be used.
   (a) The garden.
      (i) What is the significance of all the detail about who ran fastest, who went into the tomb first, what each saw, etc.? And in particular, what is the significance of the cloth that had been around Jesus' head lying separately, 'rolled up in a place by itself' (v. 7)?

   (ii) Is Jesus playing with Mary's emotions in the garden? Why does he tell her not to hold on to him (v. 17)?

(b) The upper room.

   (i) Verse 22 is John's Pentecost. What are the advantages and disadvantages of this presentation of the coming of the Holy Spirit compared with the presentation in Luke and Acts?

   (ii) Do you think Thomas touched Jesus, as he invited him to do? If he didn't, what are the implications?

   (iii) 'Jesus did many other signs . . . which are not written in this book.' What other kind of information about Jesus do you wish we had in the Gospels? Why?

(c) The lakeside.

   (i) What do you think might have been the psychological state of the disciples who decided to return to Galilee and then went fishing? What were they thinking and feeling?

   (ii) What is the significance of Peter putting on some clothes and jumping into the sea when he realized who it was on the shore (21.7)? What is John telling us?

   (iii) In their talk by the lakeside, Jesus doesn't ask Peter to grovel and say how terrible he's been. He simply asks him the question, 'Peter, do you love me?' (21.15–17). Why is this the right question to ask – both then and now?

5 **Spin-offs:**

Now may be a good time to eat something together. Jesus had fish and bread. Use your imagination to put together as varied and tasty a meal as you can devise consisting mainly of fish and bread in various guises. A glass or two of wine wouldn't do any harm! During the meal there could be a discussion (not too heavy) of how Easter impacts on members of the group, or how they have experienced Easter in the past, and how they might approach it in the future.

6 **Space for prayer:**

(a) Send each person into their own space to answer the Lord's question: 'Do you love me?' Then invite the group to reflect prayerfully on what answer we could all give to that question, and what evidence we would point to in order to back up our answer. When we've given that answer, in silence we then seek to be aware of what Jesus might say in response . . .

(b) John's account of the resurrection shows Jesus meeting people at their particular point of need: Mary needed to know she still mattered, and was called by her name; Thomas needed some convincing evidence, and was offered more than enough; Peter needed to be reinstated, and was given the opportunity to undo his three-fold denial. Suggest to the group that in silence they seek to know where their particular point of need is, and ask Christ to meet them there. Similarly, you could lead prayers for people with special areas of need, asking for the touch of Christ at those particular points.

(c) Point out that several of the accounts of the resurrection show Jesus eating with his followers – broiled fish in the upper room, the supper at Emmaus, the meal at the lake shore. Eating together seems to be a symbol of the hospitality of God and to be a foretaste of the heavenly banquet. Lead prayers for the wider Church, the local church and members of the group to be more hospitable to the outsider, the enquirer and above all to the 'little people' for whom Jesus had a special care.

7 **Ending:**
Leader: Go in the light and peace of Christ. Alleluia, alleluia!
All: **Thanks be to God. Alleluia, alleluia!**
Then blow out the candle.

Small group courses 2

FOUR RESURRECTION EVENINGS

Aim

To encourage engagement with the richness and complexity of the resurrection through different artistic media. The resurrection is so profound and mysterious that it may often be best to 'tell it slant' rather than full-on. The arts enable us to use our 'right-brain' intuitive and imaginative attributes, and thus to access other dimensions of the inexhaustible Easter message. They might also enable us to find common ground with a wider range of people, since there are many good people who cannot find their way to accepting the historical facts of Easter as the Church has believed them, but are nevertheless drawn to the deep metaphors and images of resurrection. The arts provide fertile ground for exploration together.

The resurrection in art

Materials needed

Copies of a number of representations of the resurrection as painted by artists through the centuries. There are a number of options here:

1 The paintings can be on postcards from the galleries, in art books, on slides, or even scanned into a computer for projection.

2 You may want to use as few as two or three paintings, or a wide variety. Not surprisingly, there are fewer great paintings depicting the resurrection than there are of the crucifixion. The resurrection is hard to represent without falling into naivety or parody, and fewer artists have attempted this impossible task.

3 If two or three paintings are to be taken, you could use the collection of the National Gallery, where there are to be found:
   (a) Titian: *Noli me tangere*;
   (b) Caravaggio: *The Supper at Emmaus*;
   (c) Caracci: *Domine, Quo Vadis?*
   (d) Cima: *The Incredulity of St Thomas*;
   (e) Guercino: *The Incredulity of St Thomas.*

4 You could contact someone with special artistic interest or expertise and ask them to research and produce paintings from a wider variety of sources. The internet is a good vehicle for tracking pictures down and finding background material.

The session

1 *Our backgrounds* It might be helpful to start with a general survey of the experience and interests of the group in artistic matters. Have they any training? Do they paint? Do they go to exhibitions? What painting or paintings do they remember having been particularly affected by at some stage in their lives?

2 *First painting* Introduce the first painting in whatever method you are using. The introduction should at this stage be limited to the basic facts of the painting – the artist, the date, any historical facts surrounding its painting, where it's to be found today.

3 *Responses* Some of the following questions can be used to open up discussion. Remember that the group may need to be reassured that no profound artistic knowledge or brilliance of mind is being asked for – simply honest, personal responses.
   (a) What are the first things that strike you as you look at this painting?
   (b) What techniques has the artist used to particularly good effect?
   (c) What do you think the artist might be trying to say?
   (d) What range of emotions does the painting evoke in you?
   (e) What details do you particularly notice, especially in each character?

(f) What theological issues does the painting raise? E.g. about the nature of the resurrection body.

(g) How does that painting 'carry over' into our own faith journey? Does it ask any questions of us?

4 *Expertise* It could be helpful at this stage – and not earlier! – to introduce any of the commentary which background books have to offer. For example, if you were using the National Gallery paintings you could turn to *The National Gallery Companion Guide* or to John Drury's *Painting the Word* (Yale, in association with National Gallery Publications, 1999). Both are very good value. This material would elaborate on the wisdom the group had already turned up. This is where the internet could be particularly helpful. You could also ask a minister or someone with a little theological training to offer comment at this stage on the various issues highlighted by the painting and the discussion so far.

5 *Repeat* with another painting. The added value as the session goes on is that an element of comparison will creep in as the very different styles, traditions and messages of the various paintings are thrown into relief. If only two paintings are to be discussed I would recommend the Titian and the Caravaggio. They should generate a considerable amount of discussion in the right group.

6 *Close in prayer* Use any of the prayers in the 'Stations of the resurrection' (pp. 56–62), or the prayer ideas in the small group course 'The resurrection in the Gospels' (pp. 91–102), or the section 'Prayer activities' (pp. 118–20).

The resurrection in poetry

Materials needed

The obvious materials are poems! Here, however, is a major divergence. Depending on the nature of the group, either members can be asked to bring their own favourite poems with a resurrection theme, or the leader can supply a range of poems at the session. The selection in this book might provide an initial range but the history of poetry will provide classic verse from George Herbert, John Milton, John Donne, Christina Rossetti, Gerard Manley Hopkins, R. S. Thomas and so many more. Anthologies will provide ample material, as too will the internet.[3]

If the leader is providing the poems it's best if copies can be given out so that each person is able to read and re-read the poets' precise use of words and images.

The session

1 *Our backgrounds* Again, it can be helpful to get into the subject by discussing more generally the group's experience of poetry. This is not to establish a hierarchy of expertise but simply to share members' general perception of poetry and its place in their lives. What introduced them to poetry? Do they read poetry with any degree of regularity? Which poets or poems are they particularly drawn to? Have any poems had an electrifying effect on them?

2 *First poem* This poem would either come from the first group member or from the leader's selection. All that is required before the reading of the poem is a general introduction to the poet, the date, and any particular background to the writing of the poem.

3 *Responses* Some of these questions can be used to open up discussion, while assuring members of the group that the aim isn't to impress or dazzle, but simply to share responses.

---

[3] Suitable anthologies include: *The Oxford Book of Christian Verse*, Oxford, first published 1940; *The Lion Christian Poetry Collection*, compiled by Mary Batchelor, Lion, 1995; *The Master Haunter*, compiled by David Winter, Lion, 1998.

(a) What's your immediate response to the poem, before analysis and discussion?
(b) Which phrases stand out immediately? Which do you want to savour?
(c) What is the poet trying to say and what means does he or she use to achieve that?
(d) Are there phrases or verses you think don't quite work, or you aren't quite sure you understand, or which seem ambiguous?
(e) What range of emotions does the poem evoke in you? Do any surprise you?
(f) Is this a poem you would return to?
(g) What theological issues does the poem raise for you?
(h) How might the poem 'carry over' into your own faith journey? How could it feed that journey or even subvert it?

4 *Expertise* If there is any particular expertise available to the group, either through the presence of an English teacher or someone who has done some research into the poem and the poet for this session, then now is the time to draw on that knowledge and experience. Any earlier could 'de-skill' the group, but at this point it could enrich the discussion. Similarly, if there is someone with special theological wisdom, now is the time to ask for any further reflections.

5 *Repeat* with another poem. The whole process could be speeded up or slowed down depending on the background of the group, the number of poems available, and the level of engagement the group seems to want with each poem. This is the skill of group leadership.

6 *Write your own* Greatly daring, the leader could suggest that if anyone feels inspired to attempt their own resurrection poem for the next session, it would be a great gift to the group. Some encouragement might be needed!

7 *Close with prayer* It would be very special if the prayers could come out of, and use, the poems the group has been exploring.

The resurrection in music

Materials needed

The most difficult part of this session is the preparation. It may be quite difficult to draw together recordings of a good range of different styles of Easter music. It might be necessary to put out feelers with friends and group members some time in advance. Some of the music may seem rather esoteric, but with a little patience and hard work it will hopefully come together. On the next page is a selection of possible music to try and dig out.

The session

1 *Our backgrounds* Discuss generally what styles of music members of the group enjoy. What are they enjoying at present? Who or what has been their greatest musical influence? How do people in the group use music in their lives – to listen to in the car, to play on an instrument, to work to or relax with, to go out to at concerts, etc.? Is there any music they can't stand? What kind of music makes the hair stand up on the back of their neck?

2 *Play two pieces of music on CD or tape*, inviting group members to be aware of their responses as they listen. Give a short introduction to the pieces of music, noting the composer, date and any special background to the music. In particular, be prepared to read out the words or give a copy of them to each member. Words are often difficult to make out clearly on recorded music.

3 *Responses* Some or all of these questions can be used to open up discussion. However, be aware of the power of music simply to inspire and charm; too much discussion may make the session too cerebral. Be ready to curtail discussion and just enjoy the music.
   (a) What are your immediate responses to those two pieces of music? What effect did they have on you?
   (b) Do either of the pieces of music have any special associations for you?
   (c) What did you find particularly effective or particularly irritating?

(d) How did the music and the words interact? Did they set each other off or not quite match?
(e) What range of emotions did the music evoke in you? Would this music enhance Easter for you?
(f) Would you want these pieces to be part of your musical collection?

4 *Expertise* Now is the time to draw on any particular expertise that may be available to the group. This could be in the person of a musician, music teacher or happy enthusiast. Material could be available in books or on the internet if anyone has been primed to do some research beforehand. Someone with theological ability could also be asked to reflect on the musical themes.

5 *Repeat* with two more pieces of music. Be ready to vary the amount of discussion; people might actually prefer a concert. You might also tell the group what you have available and let them make their own choices. Always be ready to remind the group that the focus is on music that portrays resurrection and helps us to respond to the glorious message of Easter.

6 *Finish* with a reflective prayer and maybe one of John Rutter's musical blessings.

A selection of Easter music

Much music is available in multiple recordings, so no recommended versions will be mentioned. Further details of other material are included below.

Classical

- Bach: 'Et resurrexit' from the B Minor Mass;
- Handel: 'I know that my Redeemer liveth' from *Messiah*;
- Mascagni: 'Easter Hymn' from *Cavalleria Rusticana*;
- Paul Spicer and Tom Wright, *Easter Oratorio*;
- Tavener: 'As one who has slept';
- Vaughan Williams: 'Easter' ('Rise, Heart, Thy Lord is Risen') from the Five Mystical Songs;

- *Easter at Canterbury*, the Choir of Canterbury Cathedral, York CD 162.

Light classical

- John Rutter: 'Christ the Lord is Risen Again';
- John Rutter: 'Agnus Dei' from the *Requiem*;
- Charles Wood (arranger): 'This Joyful Eastertide'.

Contemporary

- Adrian Snell: 'Jesus is Alive' from *The Passion*, SMCD 23;
- Graham Kendrick: 'Led Like a Lamb (You're Alive!)', on *Sacred Journey*, MWD 13;
- Graham Kendrick: 'Lord the light of your love', on *Sacred Journey*, MWD 13;
- Stuart Townend and Keith Getty: 'In Christ Alone';
- Taizé: 'Surrexit Christus' and others on CD *Resurrexit*.

Hymns

- 'Thine Be the Glory';
- 'Jesus Christ is Risen Today';
- 'Jesus Lives!';
- 'The Strife is O'er, the Battle Done';
- 'Christ the Lord is Risen Again';
- 'We Have a Gospel to Proclaim';
- 'The Day of Resurrection';
- 'Now the Green Blade Riseth'.

(The background to some of these hymns can be found in various books on hymns and their stories, available from Christian bookshops.)

The resurrection in film

The background to this session is the undeniable fact that contemporary culture is permeated by film. There are now nearly three million cinema attendances each week. The number of cinema screens in Britain nearly doubled in the last decade, and seven million 15–34-year-olds visit the cinema at least once a month. This phenomenon cries out for a Christian response. But more specifically, how has cinema handled the resurrection?

Materials needed

DVDs and videos! But what sort? There are two routes here. One is to take the way that the resurrection has been portrayed in the relatively few films in which it has been attempted. These would include Mel Gibson's *The Passion of the Christ* and Zeffirelli's *Jesus of Nazareth*, and maybe the older films *The Gospel According to St Matthew* by Pasolini or *Jesus Christ Superstar* or the evocative *Jesus of Montreal.* These are still available with a bit of searching in video shops, club catalogues or via the internet.

The other approach is the more allusive one of exploring the echoes of resurrection as a human experience in, for example, the film *Awakenings*, a true story in which mental patients in a Bronx hospital experience a remarkable resurgence of life – for a time. Other classic films raise the issue of resurrection in one way or another: *The Shawshank Redemption*, *Gladiator*, the funeral scene in *Four Weddings and a Funeral*, *Shadowlands.* Moreover, the theme is often present in the very popular genre of futuristic films such as *E.T.*, *Star Wars* and *The Matrix*, or legendary epics such as *The Lord of the Rings.*

The session

1 *Our backgrounds* Some preliminary questions about the group's experience of film will doubtless evoke a good deal more knowledge and enthusiasm than we might expect. People have longer memories and stronger views than they think. Questions such as:

(a) Which films have made the most powerful impression on you?

(b) If you could be one character from a film who would it be, and why?
(c) Has any film challenged or strengthened your faith in any way?

2 *First film* Show a clip from the first film, putting it in context. The length of the clip will depend on whether you want to explore one or two films in depth or whether you want to compare and contrast several.

3 *Responses*
(a) Some of the following questions could be asked of 'Jesus' films:
(i) What struck you about the way the resurrection was handled, if at all? If there wasn't a resurrection or none to speak of (*Jesus Christ Superstar*) how did that affect the integrity or the message of the film?
(ii) How effectively was the risen Christ portrayed? How could it have been done better?
(iii) How did the way the resurrection was presented relate to the way the rest of the gospel story was told?
(iv) Were there any insights that you gained or had reinforced through this portrayal?
(v) Is there a gospel without a resurrection?
(b) Some of the following questions could be asked in a discussion of the more 'allusive' films:
(i) Did you recognize a theme of resurrection in the film, and if so, where?
(ii) Was the experience believable? How did the characters handle such a transformation?
(iii) Was it a resurrection with a divine element of any kind, or was it a purely human experience of renewal? Is there a difference?
(iv) What feelings did the film generate in you?
(v) Does the film leave you believing such transformations are sustainable?

4 *Expertise* Increasingly there are people around who have done some serious thinking about the more profound meaning of film. If you

know of any such people (youth workers, teachers, students of film) ask them now to offer any reflections on the film and discussion so far. Other sources of deeper Christian comment can be found on the internet at <www.hollywood.com> and <www.damaris.org.uk>.

5 *Repeat* Use another film clip, or a range of them, in order to pick up the issues raised so far and to compare different ways film-makers handle the theme of resurrection and redemption.

6 You never know – a new group might emerge out of this experience, such is the energy that this kind of discussion can generate.

7 *Close with prayer* if appropriate.

Resurrection in hard places

A SELECTION OF TRUE STORIES ON AN EASTER THEME

Johannesburg under apartheid

A political rally had been cancelled by the government so Bishop Desmond Tutu offered a service inside the cathedral instead. Large numbers of riot police and armed soldiers waited outside, while inside the cathedral more police lined the walls recording everything that was said. The atmosphere was tense. Desmond Tutu declared confidently that the evil system of apartheid could not stand, and he pointed his finger at the police around the walls and said to them: 'You may be powerful, indeed very powerful, but you are not God! And the God whom we serve cannot be mocked. You have already lost!' Then he came out of the pulpit with his characteristic big smile and said, 'So, since you have already lost, we are inviting you to come and join the winning side!' The whole cathedral erupted in delight, the police left, and the congregation rose up to dance. Nothing could defeat a resurrection faith.[4]

Moscow under Communism

The then Bishop of Southwark, Mervyn Stockwood, was in Moscow over the Easter season. He went to the hairdressing salon of his hotel for a shave because his electric razor had broken. The hairdresser saw his episcopal cross and ring and asked Mervyn Stockwood if he was a bishop. He agreed that he was. The hairdresser took his cross and kissed it, and then did the same with the ring. Then, raising the razor blade aloft with his beard still on it, she called out, 'Christ is risen!'

[4] Story taken from Jim Wallis, *Faith Works*, SPCK, 2002.

whereupon the other customers joyfully responded: 'He is risen indeed. Alleluia!' Mervyn Stockwood thought to himself: 'Poor old Brezhnev [the Soviet president]: sixty years of atheism and still the Galilean conquers!'[5]

London in wartime

In 1939, when it was certain that war was on its way, the trustees of the National Gallery decided that the whole collection should be sent to Wales and then on to Canada for safety. But in the middle of the battle for France, Churchill sent a telegram to Kenneth Clark, the Director of the National Gallery, which said: 'Bury them in caves or in cellars, but not a picture shall leave these islands.' So the paintings were put into slate mines in Wales. However, two years later the public started to complain. There were daily concerts in the National Gallery but no Old Masters. A letter to *The Times* on 2 January 1942 said, 'Because London's face is scarred and bruised these days, we need more than ever to see beautiful things. Would the trustees of the National Gallery consider whether it were not wise and well to risk one picture for exhibition each week?' The trustees decided on one a month. Kenneth Clark began finding out what the public wanted and he was astonished to find that they didn't want paintings that would show re-silience or the strength of the human spirit. The picture they wanted most of all was Titian's *Noli me tangere*, a picture of the resurrection.[6]

Czechoslovakia, 1968

When the Russians went into Czechoslovakia in 1968 to put down the uprising they turned many of the great cathedrals and churches into museums. One university lecturer lost her teaching post and took a job as a cleaner in the cathedral so that the great house of God should

---

[5] Story taken from Mervyn Stockwood, *Chanctonbury Ring*, Hodder and Stoughton, 1982.

[6] From *The Times*, 5 June 2004.

continue to be prayed in. For twenty years she prayed this prayer: 'Be not afraid. Sing out for joy. Christ is risen. Alleluia.' That prayer is now sung by thousands of young people week by week in the unique Christian community at Taizé.

Uganda in the time of President Idi Amin

Thousands of people gathered on the hill called Namirembe when news came out that their archbishop Janani Luwum had been killed (by the President himself). At the funeral they had no body to mourn since the government wouldn't give the Archbishop's damaged body back. People stood around, lost. Then the former archbishop Erica Sabiti came out and began to read the story of the resurrection, particularly the passage in Luke where the angel says to the women, 'Why do you look for the living among the dead?' Gradually people realized the significance of the passage and a song of praise started up spontaneously around the hillside. 'Glory, glory, alleluia!' The message of the resurrection was striking home.

Kiev soon after the Russian Revolution

In 1920 a great atheist rally was arranged in Kiev. The powerful orator Bukharin was sent from Moscow and for an hour he attacked the Christian faith with argument, abuse and ridicule. At the end there was silence. Then questions were invited. A man rose to speak. He was a priest of the Russian Orthodox Church and he stood next to Bukharin, facing the people. He spoke just three words, using the ancient liturgical greeting for Easter Sunday. 'Christ is risen!' he declared. At once the whole crowd stood and gave the joyful response 'He is risen indeed! Alleluia!' It was a devastating moment for the atheist politician; he made no reply.

Easter in a Soviet prison camp

On Easter day all of us who were imprisoned for religious convictions were united in the one joy of Christ . . . there was no solemn Paschal service with the ringing of church bells, no possibility in our camp to gather for worship, to dress up for the festival, to prepare Easter dishes. On the contrary there was even more work and more interference than usual. All of us were surrounded by more spying, by more threats from the secret police. Yet Easter was there: great, holy, spiritual, unforgettable. It was blessed by the presence of our risen God among us – blessed by the silent Siberian stars and by our sorrows. How our hearts beat joyfully with the great Resurrection! Death is conquered, fear no more, an eternal Easter is given to us! Full of this marvellous Easter, we send you from our prison camp the victorious and joyful tidings: Christ is risen![7]

[7] From Kallistos Ware, *The Orthodox Way*, St Vladimir's Seminary Press, 1990.

Prayer activities

Prayers which focus on themes of Easter and resurrection can be found in *Common Worship: Times and Seasons*, in anthologies of prayers, liturgies from Iona and a plethora of other sources. A number of new prayers are to be found in this book, too, in the section on 'Stations of the resurrection' on pp. 56–62. What I am attempting to do in the following pages is to offer a number of prayer activities rather than actual prayers. These offer methods rather than specific content. There is another range of possibilities in the small groups course on the resurrection in the Gospels on pp. 91–102. Above all, I hope these ideas may stimulate imagination; Easter deserves our strongest prayers and our richest creativity.

1 *Opening our prayer* All occasions of prayer, either personal or public, can be started with the exchange: 'Alleluia, Christ is risen! He is risen indeed, alleluia!' It's a wonderful reminder. It can be particularly helpful in personal prayer where we may approach the time of prayer with an air of bland neutrality. The above response can truly wake us up.

2 *Praying to the risen Christ* Instead of starting prayers with the usual 'Almighty God', 'Heavenly Father' or 'Gracious God', pray 'Risen Christ . . .' Addressing our prayers in that way reminds us of the central truth in which we live – the truth of resurrection.

3 *Practising the presence of Christ* Brother Lawrence, the seventeenth-century French monk who worked in the monastery kitchen, taught us how to 'practise the presence of God'. Our Easter variation of that can be to 'practise the presence of the risen Christ'. When I was a young Christian walking back to my digs at university, I found the greatest pleasure in simply remembering the presence of a living Christ by my side. We had animated conversations and much joy.

During our ordinary days we can remember the presence of Christ, look towards him, smile, enjoy . . .

4 *The next person we meet* We can train ourselves to greet people *as Christ,* alive and before us at that moment. The truth of this is evidenced by the words of Jesus: 'just as you did it to one of the least of these . . . you did it to me' (Matt. 25.40). Christ is alive in the other people we meet day by day. The dilemma comes when we start to get practical about this. It means that the next person we meet, and the next, and the next . . . we are to treat as if they are Christ, alive before us. And this may be difficult.

5 *Christ around us* A powerful way of praying the resurrection is to use the central affirmations and prayer of 'St Patrick's Breastplate'.

> Christ be with me, Christ within me
> Christ behind me, Christ before me
> Christ beside me, Christ to win me
> Christ to comfort and restore me
>
> Christ beneath me, Christ above me
> Christ in quiet, Christ in danger
> Christ in hearts of all who love me
> Christ in mouth of friend and stranger.

Here is the calm assurance that the risen Christ is present in every dimension of our lives. We are surrounded and protected by the same risen Lord who met Mary Magdalene in the garden. It's a prayer best used at the start of the day when preparing for every eventuality.

6 *'He is going ahead of you'* Another way of praying at the start of the day is to use that phrase of the angelic messengers in the Gospels: 'He has been raised, and he is going ahead of you into Galilee; you will see him there.' We can pray in the morning: '*He has been raised, and he is going ahead of me to . . . [the day's events]: I will see him there.*' That is a theological truth in any case; God is always there ahead of us, wherever we are, but it acts as a rock of faith and hope when we're looking ahead to tricky moments coming up during the day.

7 *A symbolic movement* A flame can be lit at the start of our prayers, representing the presence of the living Christ. We may like to build on that symbolism by covering ourselves with that light. What we can do is place the tips of the fingers of both hands above the flame and then draw our fingers up to our eyes and over our head, thus covering ourselves in the light of the risen Christ. This simple action can be a powerful reminder of the presence of Christ who we receive in this way at the start of the day.

8 *Quiet meditation* The Gospel accounts of the resurrection are full of pregnant phrases that cry out for more time to mull them over and chew the goodness out of them. Here is a way to taste the goodness of these gems and let them soak into us. All we do is make ourselves comfortable, perhaps in front of a lighted candle, and drop into the gathering silence the phrase we are going to use. We repeat the phrase as often as we need, using it to draw our wandering hearts and minds back to the risen Christ. We enjoy the richness of the phrase, turning it over and over, letting it lead us into silence or into words of prayer – let the initiative be God's. Here are some phrases from the Gospel accounts of the resurrection that you might use:

(a) 'Do not be afraid.'
(b) 'Why do you look for the living among the dead?'
(c) 'He is going ahead of you.'
(d) 'My Lord and my God.'
(e) 'They worshipped him, but some doubted.'
(f) 'Were not our hearts burning within us?'
(g) 'Simon [or your own name], do you love me?'
(h) 'You are my witnesses.'

9 *Taizé Resurrexit* The Taizé CD of this name contains an hour of resurrection music from the heart of the Taizé community. This music could accompany journeys in the car, time spent in the kitchen, or dedicated time when a strong candle, or a number of nightlights, can be lit, and a longer time of peaceful reflection can be enjoyed in the company of this remarkable community where Easter is celebrated every Saturday night with great beauty and joy.

A meditation on the road to Emmaus

One powerful way of entering the Easter story is by engaging the senses, letting the mind and heart encounter the events from within. Instead of reading the story on a page, we experience it through the imagination. We see the physical environment of the story and the characters in it; we feel the night air and smell the sea; we taste the bread and the mixed herbs; we hear the conversations and the local accents; we become part of the action.

The important point is to trust the 'baptized imagination' while being careful not to drive the meditation in a particular way. We need to 'float' through the story, letting the Spirit nudge us along, rather than plod through it, working out our own agendas. God can then use this approach to enrich our understanding of the Easter events and speak directly to our hearts.

The method is simple. Read the story of the Emmaus road in Luke 24.13–35, but read it slowly and with attention, trying to notice those details you usually pass over. Read it again if necessary. Then put the Bible down, sit comfortably, close your eyes and go on a journey. What follows is an example of how a leader could conduct the journey, or the kind of mental journey an individual could take alone. If this is a led meditation, remember to leave enough time for the imagination to get to work. The temptation will be to move on too soon. Don't!

It's late afternoon and the sun is starting its long descent. You and Cleopas are trudging down the dusty road from Jerusalem. Look down the road ahead, and out at the fields around, the rough grass, the boulders, the goats. What do you notice as you look around? . . . Look down at your feet, your sandals, the rough dusty road . . . How do those feet feel on this long walk home? . . .

Be aware of Cleopas beside you, his mood, the desultory conversation, the long silences . . . What about your mood? How are you feeling? . . . Now be aware that someone else is coming up alongside. The sun is in your face; you don't look directly at him, but what are you aware of as he comes? . . . How does he ask to join you? . . . Does that feel all right? . . .

How does the conversation get going? Who says what? . . . Now Cleopas starts to tell the stranger what's been happening in Jerusalem. Listen to Cleopas' voice. Be aware of the different emotions in it . . . He speaks of Jesus, and crucifixion, and hopes dashed, and wild tales this morning from the women, and renewed confusion, and now this long walk away from it all. How does it make you feel, hearing it all again? . . .

Now the stranger starts to speak. Notice his voice; how does it sound? . . . How does it affect you? . . . He's saying some good things, things that make sense, the scriptures . . . How are you finding yourself responding to all this? What's going on inside you? . . . Look over at Cleopas. What do you see on his face? . . .

Suddenly you find you're home, in your own village. The time has gone so fast. The sun is low now; evening has nearly come. You stand by the door of your house. The stranger is already saying farewell. There's a moment of indecision. How do you feel as the stranger is about to move on? . . . One of you speaks for both; who is it? . . . You ask him in.

Be aware of the familiar contours of your house, the layout of the rooms. So much has happened since you were last here. What do you see as you look around? . . . What do you do now you're inside? And what do you ask the stranger to do? . . . What food do you and Cleopas prepare? And what drink? . . . Be aware of your mood as you get the meal ready . . .

The stranger is waiting as you enter the room where you eat. You're carrying food; you don't study his features too closely, but what do you notice about him now he's here in the house? What impressions do you have? . . . You begin to eat. Notice where each of you is sitting, how you arrange yourselves . . . The conversation continues. What is it about? The walk home? The scriptures? The weekend events in Jerusalem? . . . Listen to the others. Listen to yourself . . .

The stranger picks up bread from the plate in front of him. He raises it, thanks God for it, breaks it into three pieces, hands it out to you and Cleopas. Suddenly things begin to happen very fast. You have a strange dizzy feeling. Something is sliding into place in your head. What's going on? . . . Look over at Cleopas. What do you see on his face, and in his body? . . . Look at the stranger again. What do you see on *his* face? Can it be? . . .

You have to look away. It's all becoming too much. But when you look back towards the stranger there's no-one there! This is crazy! You feel yourself slipping. You're on your feet, looking at Cleopas. What is he doing now? . . .

Together you collapse to the floor again. Can you say anything to each other? If so, what do you say? . . . You know what you have to do. This is all madness, but you have to go back to the others, back to Jerusalem, to tell them what's happened. Is the adrenalin pumping? What do you do to get ready? . . .

Out into the night. The moon gives you light. What's going on in your heart and in your head as you start running and walking back to the city? . . . What will you say to the others? How can you make it make sense? . . . Back over the dusty road, feeling utterly different . . .

Now fast forward to the upper room where the other disciples are gathered. See the stairs, feel and hear yourself knocking on the door . . . In you go. How do you think the two of you look? . . . Who says what and how do you say it? . . . And what do the disciples say about the things that have happened to them during the day? . . .

You have to sit down. The excited conversation goes on all around you, above you. You become detached from it all. You need time to rest both the body and the brain. Rest, then. Rest in God. Be still and silent. Let God take over . . .

A week in the life of Death

This is a drama script to use in church, youth group, home group or other setting. Death sits out front with diary open and pen in hand – the script may of course be written into the diary if required. The speaker (Death) could pretend to be writing at least parts of it. The script is by David Gavin, to whom I'm grateful for permission to use it.

Death: *Monday*:
Dear Diary
It's me again – Death. Big D. What a day! Busy, busy, busy. Bit like . . . yesterday. And the day before. And the day before that.

Tragic cases really. Some so beautiful. Some so young. Oh, I nearly wept, you know . . . but in the end I didn't bother.

Well, must finish. Busy evening ahead.

Tuesday:
Dear Diary
I suppose you think it's a bit soft, Death writing a diary. But I don't really get to stop and meet anyone to chat. Oh, I meet people. I meet everyone. Met them all, the great philosophers, the great religious leaders. Great wits, great thinkers. Great twits, great stinkers. But it's all so brief and to the point. Always. ALWAYS!

Wednesday:
Dear Diary
Two big battles fought today. One in, oh . . . er . . . Thingamy and another in . . . Wherever-it-is. Now, myself, I prefer famines and plagues – then you get a good steady business over a period. Battles . . . well, you're rushed off your feet!

Making the most of the resurrection

D'you know, Diary, I can't understand these people. They spend half their time scared stiff of me and trying to avoid me, and then they have a battle! Tuh!

Thursday:

Dear Diary

(Star Trek voice) Death. The final frontier where Captain James T. Kirk must boldly go and boldly . . . go! I'm pretty impressive really, don't you think? It's the ultimate statistic, you know: one in one die . . . Yes, I like that . . . the ultimate. THE ULTIMATE.

Friday:
Dear Diary
The ultimate here. But let's not be formal about this – you can call me . . . *(thinks)* sir!

Interesting day today. A carpenter's son from Nazareth. Been a lot of fuss about him. Died well *(thoughtful)* . . . *(snaps out of it)* if you can die well! A bit like saying, 'I failed well.' A bit like saying, 'I swallow dived off a 100-foot cliff into the yawning mouth of a great white shark and got full marks for style.' *(Satisfied)* Huh!

Saturday:
Dear Diary
(Slower) Funny feeling today. Like when you've eaten something that doesn't agree with you . . . Still, death must go on! Yes, that's a much more sensible saying: 'Life must go on' – drivel! Not in my experience. Life must . . . life must grovel! *(Pause)* . . . I do feel strange.

***Sunday** – Easter Sunday – Jerusalem – Israel* AD *30*
(As if sick) Dear Diary
(Stands suddenly, looks straight ahead shocked and as if swearing) **JESUS CHRIST!** *(Curls up crying or just shaking)*

Easter poetry

Transcendence

Not for three months, let alone nine
Could Mary conceal His presence –
Nor was Joseph kept in the dark
Before His eruption like the morning star
At midnight breaking in winter –
He dazzled both shepherds and wise men:
We twelve were all blinded – three years –
Till flesh failed to veil Him, even from us,
In a calm stilled sea, and on one mountain top.
How then could we conspire to cover Him
With heavy human robes – bury Him
In puny feudal powers? Him,
Whose setting the sun mourned,
Whose light death could not extinguish?
He burst out of that grave, propelled
By resurrection – casting us all before Him
By the blaze of His uprising.

Veronica Popescu

The resurrection

I was the one who waited in the garden
Doubting the morning and the early light,
I watched the mist lift off its own soft burden,
Permitting not believing my own sight.

If there were sudden noises I dismissed
Them as a trick of sound, a sleight of hand.
Not by a natural joy could I be blessed
Or trust a thing I could not understand.

Maybe I was a shadow thrown by one
Who, weeping, came to lift away the stone,

Or was I but the path on which the sun,
Too heavy for itself, was loosed and thrown?

I heard the voices and the recognition
And love like kisses heard behind thin walls,
Were they my tears which fell, a real contrition
Or simply April with its waterfalls?

It was by negatives I learned my place.
The garden went on growing and I sensed
A sudden breeze that blew across my face.
Despair returned, but now it danced, it danced.

Elizabeth Jennings

From 'Resurrection'

The tomb, the tomb, that
Was her core and care, her one sore.
The light had hardly scarleted the dark
Or the first bird sung when Mary came in sight
With eager feet. Grief, like last night's frost,
Whitened her face and tightened all her tears.
It was there, then, there at the blinding turn
Of the bare future that she met her past.
She only heard his Angel tell her how
The holding stone broke open and gave birth
To her dear Lord, and how his shadow ran
To meet him like a dog.
And as the sun
Burns through the simmering muslins of the mist
Slowly his darkened voice, that seemed like doubt,
Morninged into noon; the summering bees
Mounted and boiled over in the bell-flowers.
'Come out of your jail, Mary,' he said, 'the doors are open
and joy has its ear cocked for your coming.
Earth now is no place to mope in. So throw away
Your doubt, cast every clout of care,
Hang all your hallelujahs out
This airy day.'

W. R. Rodgers

Seven stanzas for Easter

Make no mistake: if He rose at all
it was as His body;
if the cells' dissolution did not reverse, the molecules
reknit, the amino acids rekindle,
the Church will fall.

It was not the flowers,
each soft Spring recurrent;
it was not as His Spirit in the mouths and fuddled
eyes of the eleven apostles;
it was as His flesh: ours.

The same hinged thumbs and toes,
the same valved heart
that – pierced – died, withered, paused, and then
regathered out of enduring Might
new strength to enclose.

Let us not mock God with metaphor,
analogy, sidestepping, transcendence;
making of the event a parable, a sign painted in the
faded credulity of earlier ages:
let us walk through the door.

The stone is rolled back, not papier-mâché,
not a stone in a story,
but the vast rock of materiality that in the slow
grinding of time will eclipse for each of us
the wide light of day.

And if we will have an angel at the tomb,
make it a real angel,
weighty with Max Planck's quanta, vivid with hair,
opaque in the dawn light, robed in real linen
spun on a definite loom.

Let us not seek to make it less monstrous,
for our own convenience, or own sense of beauty,
lest, awakened in one unthinkable hour, we are
embarrassed by the miracle,
and crushed by remonstrance.

John Updike

Easter St John

God so loved he gave
God loved so he gave
God loved, he gave so.

So teach me to love;
So I may love, I'll give,
So I may give, I'll love,
I may so love to give.

Teach me Lord to give,
And loving give, and giving love.
So Thou be gift and love so.

Ruth Etchells

Poem for Easter

Tell me:
What came first
Easter or the egg?
Crucifixion
  or daffodils?
Three days in a tomb
  or four days
In Paris?
  (returning
Bank Holiday Monday).

When is a door
Not a door?
When it is rolled away.
When is a body
Not a body?
When it is a risen.

Question.
Why was it the Saviour
Rode on the cross?
Answer
To get us
To the other side.

Behold I stand.
Behold I stand and what?
Behold I stand at the door and
Knock knock.

Steve Turner

Deleted

Deleted! That Friday
Saw off another in the long
Series of Meddlers.
Messiah?
Not likely.
Never been,
Still to come,
Whenever . . .

Deleted! That Grim Friday
Sawed away the life
Of God.
Almighty?
Not likely.
Never been,
A God who died,
Ever.

Deleted! That Good Friday
Saw off the power of death
Itself.
Unattainable?
Not likely.
God's given life
For-given-ness,
Life for ever.

David Grieve

Eastering

To find an Eastering place,
And hear the grating sound of shifting stone,
And imagine beating wings in every fragile noise,
And measure his vacated bed.

To make anywhere his Eastering place,
And make matter hallowed ground
Because it was so for him.

To give free spirit a location,
A starting point, a focus,
Because I am flesh too,
And it matters.

David Grieve

Resurrection

All day in darkness,
folded in stone,
he was unable to move,
restricted by death,
as well as grave clothes.

Wakened by footsteps
outside or perhaps the noise
of bones setting themselves for a fight.
He pushed against the homespun linen shroud –
found himself outside himself for a while.

Pushing against the stone,
folding it as easy as the linen,
he stood outside
and listened to the sound
of his heart beat.
Flexing the muscles in his arms.

Val Shedden

Next time

If hearing is the last sense we lose in life
will it be the first to return
at the call of the trumpet?

The first call not quite audible
we may lie in the dark
waiting, unsure of the newness of it all.
Having lain so long silent
we will inhale slowly,
savouring the coolness,
holding our breath before choosing
carefully,

which word to say first
– this time.

Val Shedden

That Nature is a Heraclitean Fire and of the Comfort of the Resurrection

Extract

Enough! the Resurrection,
A heart's-clarion! Away grief's gasping, joyless days, dejection.
  Across my foundering deck shone
A beacon, an eternal beam. Flesh fade, and mortal trash
Fall to the residuary worm; world's wildfire, leave but ash:
  In a flash, at a trumpet crash,
I am all at once what Christ is, since he was what I am, and
This Jack, joke, poor potsherd, patch, matchwood, immortal diamond,
  Is immortal diamond.

Gerard Manley Hopkins

And finally . . .

God,
Resurrection.
Wow!
Amen.

Appendix 1

THE FOUR GOSPEL ACCOUNTS OF THE RESURRECTION

Matthew

28 [1]After the sabbath, as the first day of the week was dawning, Mary
Magdalene and the other Mary went to see the tomb. [2]And suddenly
there was a great earthquake; for an angel of the Lord, descending
from heaven, came and rolled back the stone and sat on it. [3]His
appearance was like lightning, and his clothing white as snow. [4]For fear
of him the guards shook and became like dead men. [5]But the angel
said to the women, 'Do not be afraid: I know that you are looking for
Jesus who was crucified. [6]He is not here; for he has been raised, as he
said. Come, see the place where he lay. [7]Then go quickly and tell his
disciples, "He has been raised from the dead, and indeed he is going
ahead of you to Galilee; there you will see him." This is my message to
you.' [8]So they left the tomb quickly with fear and great joy, and ran to
tell his disciples. [9]Suddenly Jesus met them and said, 'Greetings!' And
they came to him, took hold of his feet, and worshipped him. [10]Then
Jesus said to them, 'Do not be afraid; go and tell my brothers to go to
Galilee; there they will see me.'

[11]While they were going, some of the guard went into the city and
told the chief priests everything that had happened. [12]After the priests
had assembled with the elders, they devised a plan to give a large sum
of money to the soldiers, [13]telling them, 'You must say, "His disciples
came by night and stole him away while we were asleep." [14]If this
comes to the governor's ears, we will satisfy him and keep you out of
trouble.' [15]So they took the money and did as they were directed. And
this story is still told among the Jews to this day.

[16]Now the eleven disciples went to the Galilee, to the mountain to
which Jesus had directed them. [17]When they saw him, they worshipped
him; but some doubted. [18]And Jesus came and said to them, 'All

authority in heaven and on earth has been given to me. [19]Go therefore and make disciples of all nations, baptizing them in the name of the Father and of the Son and of the Holy Spirit, [20]and teaching them to obey everything that I have commanded you. And remember, I am with you always, to the end of the age.'

Mark

16 [1]When the sabbath was over, Mary Magdalene, and Mary the mother of James, and Salome bought spices, so that they might go and anoint him. [2]And very early on the first day of the week, when the sun had risen, they went to the tomb. [3]They had been saying to one another, 'Who will roll away the stone for us from the entrance to the tomb?' [4]When they looked up, they saw that the stone, which was very large, had already been rolled back. [5]As they entered the tomb, they saw a young man, dressed in a white robe, sitting on the right side; and they were alarmed. [6]But he said to them, 'Do not be alarmed; you are looking for Jesus of Nazareth, who was crucified. He has been raised; he is not here. Look, there is the place they laid him. [7]But go, tell his disciples and Peter that he is going ahead of you to Galilee; there you will see him, just as he told you.' [8]So they went out and fled from the tomb, for terror and amazement had seized them; and they said nothing to anyone, for they were afraid.

The shorter ending of Mark

[And all that had been commanded them they told briefly to those around Peter. And afterwards Jesus himself sent out through them, from east to west, the sacred and imperishable proclamation of eternal salvation.]

The longer ending of Mark

[9][Now after he rose early on the first day of the week, he appeared first to Mary Magdalene, from whom he had cast out seven demons. [10]She went out and told those who had been with him, while they were mourning and weeping. [11]But when they heard that he was alive and had been seen by her, they would not believe it.

12After this he appeared in another form to two of them, as they were walking into the country. 13And they went back and told the rest, but they did not believe them.

14Later he appeared to the eleven themselves as they were sitting at the table; and he upbraided them for their lack of faith and stubbornness, because they had not believed those who saw him after he had risen. 15And he said to them, 'Go into all the world and proclaim the good news to the whole creation. 16The one who believes and is baptized will be saved; but the one who does not believe will be condemned. 17And these signs will accompany those who believe: by using my name they will cast out demons; they will speak in new tongues; 18they will pick up snakes in their hands, and if they drink any deadly thing, it will not hurt them; they will lay their hands on the sick, and they will recover.'

19So then the Lord Jesus, after he had spoken to them, was taken up into heaven and sat down at the right hand of God. 20And they went out and proclaimed the good news everywhere, while the Lord worked with them and confirmed the message by the signs that accompanied it.]

Luke

24 1But on the first day of the week, at early dawn, they came to the tomb, taking the spices that they had prepared. 2They found the stone rolled away from the tomb, 3but when they went in, they did not find the body. 4While they were perplexed about this, suddenly two men in dazzling clothes stood beside them. 5The women were terrified and bowed their faces to the ground, but the men said to them, 'Why do you look for the living among the dead? He is not here, but has risen. 6Remember how he told you, while he was still in Galilee, 7that the Son of Man must be handed over to sinners, and be crucified, and on the third day rise again.' 8Then they remembered his words, 9and returning from the tomb, they told all this to the eleven and to all the rest. 10Now it was Mary Magdalene, Joanna, Mary the mother of James, and the other women with them who told this to the apostles. 11But these words seemed to them an idle tale, and they did not believe them.

12But Peter got up and ran to the tomb; stooping and looking in, he saw the linen cloths by themselves; then he went home, amazed at what had happened.

13Now on that same day two of them were going to a village called Emmaus, about seven miles from Jerusalem, 14and talking with each other about all these things that had happened. 15While they were talking and discussing, Jesus himself came near and went with them, 16but their eyes were kept from recognizing him. 17And he said to them, ‘What are you discussing with each other while you walk along?’ They stood still, looking sad. 18Then one of them, whose name was Cleopas, answered him, ‘Are you the only stranger in Jerusalem who does not know the things that have taken place there in these days?’

19He asked them, ‘What things?’ They replied, ‘The things about Jesus of Nazareth, who was a prophet mighty in deed and word before God and all the people, 20and how our chief priests and leaders handed him over to be condemned to death and crucified him. 21But we had hoped that he was the one to redeem Israel. Yes, and besides all this, it is now the third day since these things took place. 22Moreover, some women of our group astounded us. They were at the tomb early this morning, 23and when they did not find his body there, they came back and told us that they had indeed seen a vision of angels who said that he was alive. 24Some of those who were with us went to the tomb and found it just as the women had said; but they did not see him.’ 25Then he said to them, ‘Oh, how foolish you are, and how slow of heart to believe all that the prophets have declared! 26Was it not necessary that the Messiah should suffer these things and then enter into his glory?’ 27Then beginning with Moses and all the prophets, he interpreted to them the things about himself in all the scriptures.

28As they came near the village to which they were going, he walked ahead as if he were going on. 29But they urged him strongly, saying, ‘Stay with us, because it is almost evening and the day is now nearly over.’ So he went in to stay with them. 30When he was at the table with them, he took bread, blessed and broke it, and gave it to them. 31Then their eyes were opened, and they recognized him; and he vanished from their sight. 32They said to each other, ‘Were not our hearts burning within us while he was talking to us on the road, while he was

opening the scriptures to us?' 33That same hour they got up and returned to Jerusalem; and they found the eleven and their companions
gathered together. 34They were saying, 'The Lord has risen indeed, and
he has appeared to Simon!' 35Then they told what had happened on
the road, and how he had been made known to them in the breaking
of the bread.

36While they were talking about this, Jesus himself stood among
them and said to them, 'Peace be with you.' 37They were startled and
terrified, and thought that they were seeing a ghost. 38He said to them,
'Why are you frightened, and why do doubts arise in your hearts?
39Look at my hands and my feet; see that it is I myself. Touch me and
see; for a ghost does not have flesh and bones as you see that I have.'
40And when he had said this, he showed them his hands and his feet.
41While in their joy they were disbelieving and still wondering, he said
to them, 'Have you anything here to eat?' 42They gave him a piece of
broiled fish, 43and he took it and ate in their presence.

44Then he said to them, 'These are my words that I spoke to you
while I was still with you – that everything written about me in the law
of Moses, the prophets and the psalms must be fulfilled.' 45Then he
opened their minds to understand the scriptures, 46and he said to them,
'Thus it is written, that the Messiah is to suffer and to rise from the
dead on the third day, 47and that repentance and forgiveness of sins is
to be proclaimed in his name to all nations, beginning from Jerusalem.
48You are witnesses of these things. 49And see, I am sending upon you
what my Father promised; so stay here in the city until you have been
clothed with power from on high.'

50Then he led them out as far as Bethany, and, lifting up his hands,
he blessed them. 51While he was blessing them, he withdrew from
them and was carried up into heaven. 52And they worshipped him, and
returned to Jerusalem with great joy; 53and they were continually in the
temple blessing God.

John

20 1Early on the first day of the week, while it was still dark, Mary
Magdalene came to the tomb and saw that the stone had been removed

from the tomb. 2So she ran and went to Simon Peter and the other disciple, the one whom Jesus loved, and said to them, 'They have taken the Lord out of the tomb, and we do not know where they have laid him.' 3Then Peter and the other disciple set out and went towards the tomb. 4The two were running together, but the other disciple outran Peter and reached the tomb first. 5He bent down to look in and saw the linen wrappings lying there, but he did not go in. 6Then Simon Peter came, following him, and went into the tomb. He saw the linen wrappings lying there, 7and the cloth that had been on Jesus' head, not lying with the linen wrappings but rolled up in a place by itself. 8Then the other disciple, who reached the tomb first, also went in, and he saw and believed; 9for as yet they did not understand the scripture, that he must rise from the dead. 10Then the disciples returned to their homes.

11But Mary stood weeping outside the tomb. As she wept, she bent over to look into the tomb; 12and she saw two angels in white, sitting where the body of Jesus had been lying, one at the head and the other at the feet. 13They said to her, 'Woman, why are you weeping?' She said to them, 'They have taken away my Lord, and I do not know where they have laid him.' 14When she had said this, she turned around and saw Jesus standing there, but she did not know that it was Jesus. 15Jesus said to her, 'Woman, why are you weeping? Whom are you looking for?' Supposing him to be the gardener, she said to him, 'Sir, if you have carried him away, tell me where you have laid him, and I will take him away.' 16Jesus said to her, 'Mary!' She turned and said to him in Hebrew, 'Rabbouni!' (which means Teacher). 17Jesus said to her, 'Do not hold on to me, because I have not yet ascended to the Father. But go to my brothers and say to them, "I am ascending to my Father and your Father, to my God and your God."' 18Mary Magdalene went and announced to the disciples, 'I have seen the Lord'; and she told them that he had said these things to her.

19When it was evening on that day, the first day of the week, and the doors of the house where the disciples had met were locked for fear of the Jews, Jesus came and stood among them and said, 'Peace be with you.' 20After he said this, he showed them his hands and his side. Then the disciples rejoiced when they saw the Lord. 21Jesus said to them

again, 'Peace be with you. As the Father has sent me, so I send you.'
[22]When he had said this, he breathed on them and said to them, 'Receive the Holy Spirit. [23]If you forgive the sins of any, they are forgiven
them; if you retain the sins of any, they are retained.'

[24]But Thomas (who was called the Twin), one of the twelve, was not
with them when Jesus came. [25]So the other disciples told him, 'We
have seen the Lord.' But he said to them, 'Unless I see the marks of the
nails in his hands, and put my finger in the marks of the nails and my
hand in his side, I will not believe.'

[26]A week later his disciples were again in the house, and Thomas was
with them. Although the doors were shut, Jesus came and stood among
them and said, 'Peace be with you.' [27]Then he said to Thomas, 'Put
your finger here and see my hands. Reach out your hand and put it in
my side. Do not doubt but believe.' [28]Thomas answered him, 'My Lord
and my God!' [29]Jesus said to him, 'Have you believed because you have
seen me? Blessed are those who have not seen and yet have come to
believe.'

[30]Now Jesus did many other signs in the presence of his disciples,
which are not written in this book. [31]But these are written so that you
may come to believe that Jesus is the Messiah, the Son of God, and that
through believing you may have life in his name.

21 [1]After these things Jesus showed himself again to the disciples by the
Sea of Tiberias; and he showed himself in this way. [2]Gathered there
together were Simon Peter, Thomas called the Twin, Nathanael of
Cana in Galilee, the sons of Zebedee, and two others of his disciples.
[3]Simon Peter said to them, 'I am going fishing.' They said to him, 'We
will go with you.' They went out and got into the boat, but that night
they caught nothing.

[4]Just after daybreak, Jesus stood on the beach; but the disciples did
not know that it was Jesus. [5]Jesus said to them, 'Children, you have no
fish, have you?' They answered him, 'No.' [6]He said to them, 'Cast the
net to the right side of the boat, and you will find some.' So they cast it,
and now they were not able to haul it in because there were so many
fish. [7]That disciple whom Jesus loved said to Peter, 'It is the Lord!'
When Simon Peter heard that it was the Lord, he put on some clothes,

for he was naked, and jumped into the sea. 8But the other disciples
came in the boat, dragging the net full of fish, for they were not far
from the land, only about a hundred yards off.

9When they had gone ashore, they saw a charcoal fire there, with
fish on it, and bread. 10Jesus said to them, 'Bring some of the fish that
you have just caught.' 11So Simon Peter went aboard and hauled the
net ashore, full of large fish, a hundred and fifty-three of them; and
though there were so many, the net was not torn. 12Jesus said to them,
'Come and have breakfast.' Now none of the disciples dared to ask
him, 'Who are you?' because they knew it was the Lord. 13Jesus came
and took the bread and gave it to them, and did the same with the fish.
14This was now the third time that Jesus appeared to the disciples after
he was raised from the dead.

15When they had finished breakfast, Jesus said to Simon Peter, 'Simon
son of John, do you love me more than these?' He said to him, 'Yes,
Lord; you know that I love you.' Jesus said to him, 'Feed my lambs.'
16A second time he said to him, 'Simon son of John, do you love me?'
He said to him, 'Yes, Lord; you know that I love you.' Jesus said to
him, 'Tend my sheep.' 17He said to him the third time, 'Simon son of
John, do you love me?' Peter felt hurt because he said to him the third
time, 'Do you love me?' And he said to him, 'Lord, you know everything; you know that I love you.' Jesus said to him, 'Feed my sheep.
18Very truly, I tell you, when you were younger, you used to fasten
your own belt and to go wherever you wished. But when you grow old,
you will stretch out your hands, and someone else will fasten a belt
around you and take you where you do not wish to go.' 19(He said this
to indicate the kind of death by which he would glorify God.) After
this he said to him, 'Follow me.'

20Peter turned and saw the disciple whom Jesus loved following
them: he was the one who had reclined next to Jesus at the supper and
had said, 'Lord, who is it that is going to betray you?' 21When Peter saw
him, he said to Jesus, 'Lord, what about him?' 22Jesus said to him, 'If it
is my will that he remain until I come, what is that to you? Follow me!'
23So the rumour spread in the community that this disciple would not
die. Yet Jesus did not say to him that he would not die, but, 'If it is my
will that he remain until I come, what is that to you?'

24 This is the disciple who is testifying to these things and has written
them, and we know that his testimony is true. 25 But there are also
many other things that Jesus did; if every one of them were written
down, I suppose that the world itself could not contain the books that
would be written.

Appendix 2

FURTHER RESOURCES

Books

Stephen T. Davis, *Risen Indeed: Making Sense of the Resurrection*, SPCK, 1993.
An examination at the interface of theology, philosophy and biblical studies.

John V. Taylor, *The Easter God, and His Easter People*, Continuum, 2003.
A collection of sermons illuminating various aspects of a resurrection faith.

Peter Walker, *The Weekend that Changed the World*, Marshall Pickering, 1999.
Explores the history, location and meaning of the first Easter.

Rowan Williams, *Resurrection: Interpreting the Easter Gospel*, DLT, 2002.
How the experience of the resurrection is fundamentally about forgiveness and healing.

N. T. Wright, *The Resurrection of the Son of God*, SPCK, 2003.
The 'big book' that argues everything there is to argue about in Tom Wright's typically vigorous and readable style.

N. T. Wright and Marcus Borg, *The Meaning of Jesus*, SPCK, 1999.
In Part 4 the authors explore the resurrection in significantly different ways – a valuable model of debate.

DVDs and videos

The Gospel According to St Matthew Pasolini's Marxist vision of Jesus as a political figure. An old but classic film in black and white with quite a punch.

Jesus Christ Superstar Based on the Andrew Lloyd Webber/Tim Rice musical, this film has no resurrection to speak of but is worth seeing again for its strange power and strong music.

Jesus of Montreal A fascinating contemporary retelling of the story. You either go with it or you don't!

Jesus of Nazareth The Franco Zeffirelli TV film with Robert Powell as Jesus, which many people found the most memorable attempt to achieve the impossible.

The Lion, the Witch and the Wardrobe The BBC film of the classic story by C. S. Lewis in which Aslan, the great lion, represents Christ. Enchanting and powerful.

Lumen Christi: the Risen Christ Taizé video, 2000; 45 mins. Interleaves Easter celebrations at Taizé with a theologian's comments and reflections. Both gentle and stimulating.

The Mysteries Heritage Theatre Video, 1998. The South African touring production shown also on BBC television. The whole Bible story, but with a very effective ending. Brilliant.

The Passion of the Christ Icon DVD. Mel Gibson's electrifying, terrifying account of the last twelve hours of the life of Jesus, with an intriguing short sequence of the resurrection.

Tales from the Madhouse BBC/Bible Society. Eight striking monologues from various characters involved in the Easter story. Excellent discussion starters; 15 mins each.